UNLEASHING
THE POWER OF
CONFIRMATION

BY ALISON GRISWOLD

◯ LIFE TEEN

Designed by Casey Olson.

Authored by Alison Griswold.

Copy editing by Natalie Tansill and Claudia Volkman.

ISBN: 978-0-9915965-1-5

Copyright ©2014 Life Teen, Inc. All rights reserved.

Published by Life Teen, Inc.
2222 S. Dobson Rd.
Suite 601
Mesa, AZ 85202

LifeTeen.com
Printed in the United States of America.
Printed on acid-free paper.

For more information about Life Teen or to order additional copies, go online to LifeTeen.com or call us at 1-800-809-3902.

FOR MOM AND DAD.

TABLE OF CONTENTS

INTRODUCTION

When I was six, I received the board game Mousetrap for my birthday. If you've never had the opportunity to play this game, I'm so sorry. Turn off your iDevice and search the attic — maybe you'll luck out and find a box containing this awesome contraption. The game involves assembling a board that is a combination of marbles falling, seesaws flipping, rubber bands snapping and even a little plastic guy flipping backwards into a barrel of cardboard cheese.

I excitedly opened the box and attempted to set up the mousetrap. I managed to get some of the pieces to work but began to realize that my chubby six-year-old fingers weren't dexterous enough to assemble the more minute parts of the game. I couldn't get the rubber band into the tiny notch that would snap back to knock over a bucket. The plastic cage that would lower onto the plastic mice was easily jarred by my elbow hitting the board when I reached over to roll the dice and was constantly lowering *before* the mice arrived.

Lame.

This game would require the assistance of an adult, which in my mind made it infinitely less fun, and the "ages six and up" label was now an infuriating example of false advertising. Disappointed, I kicked the box under my bed and went back to the simpler task of brushing Barbie's hair so she could meet Ken for a ride in the dune buggy. The Mousetrap box remained under my bed. Unused. Unplayed. It had been exciting to receive, but it ended up just collecting dust when I realized I wasn't able to use it.

When we receive the Sacrament of Confirmation, it can be a lot like the day I received Mousetrap. The *Catechism of the Catholic Church* explains that one of the effects of the sacrament is that it "increases the gifts of the Holy Spirit" in us (*CCC* 1303), but if we don't understand how to use the gifts or think that they're for us to use when we get older, we miss out on a lot of help they can offer us right now.

The good news is that if you've been baptized, you have already received the gifts of the Holy Spirit. If you've received the Sacrament of Confirmation, these gifts have increased in your soul. It doesn't matter if you remember, understand, or even sent a thank-you note for the Bible your grandma gave you on that day. You *have* the gifts of the Holy Spirit.

But are you using them?

When it comes to God as Father, Son, and Holy Spirit (one God in three persons — check out paragraph 253 of the *Catechism* for more on this), we can be a lot more confident about understanding how God the Father and Son work in our lives. We all have at least a vague idea of the role of a father, since while God "transcends human fatherhood and motherhood... He is their origin and standard" (*CCC* 239). We may struggle with our understanding of God as heavenly Father because of our experiences with our earthly parents, but we at least have an idea to begin from when we're seeking to understand God the Father.

We know God the Son through the accounts of His life in the Gospels. Many find Christ much easier to relate to simply because He became one of us. When I read about the life of Christ from St. Matthew, St. Mark, St. Luke, and St. John, I may not know what it was like to walk on water or feed 5,000 people, but I can at least begin to imagine what it would have looked like and how people would have reacted.

The Holy Spirit can seem a lot more mysterious.

Maybe you hear "Holy Spirit" and remember the story of Pentecost, when the apostles were gathered in the Upper Room and tongues of fire descended upon them. Or maybe you've seen people on Sunday morning television, praying enthusiastically for the Holy Spirit to fill a room full of church ladies with big hats, waving fans and singing gospel songs.

You're not preaching in Jerusalem and you don't wear a big church-lady hat (well, maybe you do. And that's OK). You're a student, a son or daughter, a brother or sister, a friend and a teammate. Yet the gifts of the Holy Spirit were given to you at your Baptism, have been (or will be) strengthened through your Confirmation and basically are for everyone, right now. In fact, the *Catechism* goes so far as to say that our moral life is "sustained" by the gifts of the Holy Spirit (see *CCC* 1830). To be moral is to do what's right, and to be "sustained" by something is to be totally dependent on it. Therefore, we depend on the gifts of the Holy Spirit to do what's right.

As you learn about them, you'll probably realize that you're already using these gifts. However, the more aware you are of what you have, the better you'll be able to put them to use.

The chapters that follow break down each gift of the Holy Spirit with an example or illustration of what it would look like in real life, an explanation of what it is and some ways to use it more effectively in your life. Think of this as a "user's manual" for all you received at your Confirmation.

I was too young to enjoy Mousetrap, but you are not too young for what you were given at your Baptism and Confirmation. Don't kick your spiritual life under the bed and think you'll revisit it when you're in college or married or old enough to rent a car. These gifts are for you right here, right now.

The seven gifts of the Spirit come from Isaiah 11:1-3: wisdom, understanding, knowledge, counsel, piety, fortitude, and fear of the Lord (see *CCC* 1831). These were the traits of the shoot that would come "from the stump of Jesse" (Isaiah 11:1), traits that would be a sign of the Messiah. If this is how we would recognize Christ, it is also how others will recognize Christ in us.

Read on. Learn that you've been gifted.

WISDOM

−REAL LIFE−

In the parish my family attended, the youth group was pretty informal. You could start attending in seventh or eighth grade, but you couldn't go on summer trips until you were in high school. Those of us who joined as middle schoolers had to endure two years of stories of summer adventures before we could participate ourselves. Looking back, it was pretty shrewd marketing. We saw slideshows of the trip to see the pope at World Youth Day and looked with envy at the diocesan youth conference T-shirts that were signed by all the new friends they made who lived hours away.

Most mysterious to us, though, were the stories from work camp. Wildly popular, this trip involved going to some faraway land for a week where everyone would sleep on the floor of school classrooms, take cold showers, and repair houses for the needy in the community. Our friends would come home covered in paint primer that wouldn't scrub off in the cold water. They also had gross blisters and peeling sunburns from spending all day outside hammering, raking, and painting.

To us middle schoolers, this was the trip that we couldn't wrap our minds around. What was so appealing about all that work? It was summer and our beach town afforded us some pretty sweet options when school let out. We could spend our days in the ocean, poolside, or making money at one of the many shops and restaurants that needed summer help. How was it that our friends were having so much fun driving to some Podunk town and sweating for a week?

When we were finally old enough and registrations for that summer's work camp in Orlando were passed out, the older students started laying on the peer pressure when they saw us hesitating at the thought of working in the Florida sun all week.

"Everyone's going. You better sign up, Griz. Besides, you are pale. A week in Florida will only help you. You look like a ghost."

My friends didn't fall for the "persuade through flattery" route.

In the end, I did sign up. There were three things that contributed to this decision: pressure from my older friends whom I really looked up to, the thought that this was a chance to serve people who needed help, and the realization that this was a week without my parents or siblings. I loved my family, but I was 14 and the thought of freedom — even if it cost me sleeping on the floor and cold showers — was pretty enticing.

After I turned in my registration and deposit, I lay awake that night as my mind raced through all the reasons this was not a good idea after all. A whole week away from home — what was I thinking? What if I got carsick and threw up in the car? What if my friends didn't talk to me? What if I didn't like the people I met there? What if they didn't like me? What if there were no curtains on the shower — or worse, no doors on the toilet stalls? What if they only served runny eggs for breakfast? I hated runny eggs. What if I wore the wrong clothes, said the wrong things, and couldn't stop laughing at a joke that wasn't funny and everyone stared at me?

These fears nagged me but I didn't give in, and a warm Sunday in June found me in a 13-passenger van — squished between my friends, paintbrushes, and sleeping bags — cruising down Interstate 95, bound for Orlando, Florida. Just as we had been warned, our accommodations were the linoleum floor of a classroom, and the showers were not only cold but also on the other side of the building. But there were curtains, doors, and pizza... so I felt myself begin to calm down.

I was assigned to Team 17. Our group of six was given a sheet with our work assignment on it: the home of an elderly woman, Miss Betty, who lived in one of the sprawling neighborhoods on the outskirts of town. We were supposed to clean her yard, paint her walls, caulk her tub, and install a sink.

Wait. *Install a sink?* We were high schoolers, not Joe the Plumber. They must have us mixed up with someone else. I felt the butterflies flooding my stomach again. Not knowing how to install a sink hadn't even occurred to me as something to worry about, but looking at the supplies our team had been handed, we now had 99 problems — and building a sink was one of them.

We pulled up to Miss Betty's home the next morning and were met by a yard full of not just lawn debris but empty cans, bottles, a broken lawn mower, discarded books, broken porcelain figurines, and a fence that had fallen down. When we entered her house, every surface was covered with layers of random stuff and it smelled like burnt baked beans.

Miss Betty welcomed us, smiling, but looked as uncertain as I felt. "You all done this before?" she asked.

"No!" I wanted to say. "I'm just 14 and I've only ever painted by number in art class!" Before I blurted out what was on my mind, our team leader suggested we begin with prayer. We were sure going to need it.

Next the jobs were divided up. The guys were assigned the scraping and sanding on the walls of the house to prep for painting. "Alison and Amanda," our team leader said, gesturing for us to come over. "You girls look meticulous and good at following directions. Why don't you start putting the new sink together?"

Amanda was a sophomore, so she had that on me. However, she looked just as confounded by the idea of building a sink as I did. "Uh... we..." we both began. "I know it looks like a lot," our leader assured us, "but it isn't that hard. The tools are all included in the box. You just need to read the directions one step at a time. Just try it — I'll be right outside if you need help."

Amanda looked at me. "I've never built *anything*," she confessed. As a kid, I had been pretty good with Legos, but I wasn't about to admit that to a girl who was older and tanner than me.

"Me neither," I said.

"Well," she said dubiously, "I guess we have to try."

3

We opened the box and pulled out the plastic bags with the screws, grommets, nails, and pieces that would make up the base of the sink. Finding the beginning of the directions, step-by-step we put the pieces where instructed. Although we had to take a break to ask how we were supposed to get Phillip's screwdriver when he wasn't even on our team, we plodded away under the Florida sun, and about an hour and a half later, we had assembled the base of a sink. And we now knew the difference between a Phillips and flat-head screwdriver.

I was pleased as punch. I had woven potholders, braided friendship bracelets, and built birdhouses out of Popsicle sticks, but never had I ever made something as useful or important as the base of a sink for someone who had an exposed pipe where a sink needed to be. After posing for pictures in front of it, Amanda and I carried it into Miss Betty's bathroom. We screwed in a few pipes, caulked the corners and boom: Let there be sink.

Miss Betty came into her bathroom and saw her brand-new sink, complete with a door that opened to reveal a cabinet for storage. It gleamed white and new in her home. It wasn't just a sink; it was a sign of hope in a house that had previously looked forgotten and neglected under layers of dust and knickknacks. Miss Betty was elated — I don't think she had expected us to accomplish this, much less before lunch on Monday. I know I sure hadn't. As she hugged Amanda and me, it clicked. I understood why work camp was so popular. Why my friends looked forward to it every year, and why they were so adamant that I sign up that year.

I could have been at the pool or beach that morning, but winning Marco Polo and getting pruney hands and feet didn't feel nearly as amazing as looking at the sink in Miss Betty's bathroom and realizing that Amanda and I had given her not just a new bathroom fixture, but the knowledge that people cared about her.

The rest of the week was no cakewalk. Ironically, assembling the sink was one of the easier projects we took on. Donning heavy gloves, we weeded through all the trash in the front yard and sweated buckets while we hauled the broken figurines, cans, glasses, and old lawn mower away. We fixed the fence. We painted her house a bright turquoise and hot pink (Miss Betty's choice), and we learned from talking to her that she had once owned an antique shop but had to close it to take care of her grandchildren. The remnants now lined her shelves and tables.

I returned home that Saturday with the blisters, paint stains, and sunburn that my friends had been sporting after work camps for years. I wouldn't have traded that week for anything, though. My first week away from my parents had been full of choices — choosing to get in the van, choosing to cooperate with Amanda to try and build the sink, choosing to pray with my group, choosing to get to know Miss Betty, choosing to be open to what each day held. I could have chosen not to go or chosen to just sit on the lawn next to the broken lawn mower, convinced that the task at hand was too hard. But I hadn't, and I was a better person for it.

What had guided these choices?

—APPLICATION—

If I told you that God is real, heaven exists and you were created to spend eternity there, this would probably not be news to you. Even if you haven't been to Sunday school in a really long time, you probably remember the basics. God created Adam and Eve, and when they chose to disobey Him by eating from the one tree that God forbade them to eat from, original sin entered the world and we were cut off from heaven. But God loved us all too much to leave us separated from Him, and He had a plan to fix the separation caused by Adam and Eve. Scripture tells us this, explaining "when the time had fully come, God sent His Son, born of a woman, born under the law, to redeem those who were under the law, so that we might receive adoption as sons" (Galatians 4:4–5). Let the gravity of this sink in: God became man so the break caused by the sin of Adam and Eve could be mended. He is God, but He took on all the stuff that we suffer through here on earth — cold weather, blisters, and moldy bananas — to meet us right where we are.

Maybe you've heard this story of God becoming one of us so often that you take it for granted — it's a fact, just like the sky being blue and water being wet. We sometimes think of people who know lots of facts as being wise or having lots of wisdom, but it's not quite the same thing as wisdom as a gift of the Holy Spirit. In the Old Testament, we are familiar with the story of King David (think David and Goliath), but it is his son and successor Solomon who paints a picture of wisdom in action. God appears to Solomon and asks him what God can give him (see 2 Chronicles 1:7). Solomon replies, "Give me now wisdom and knowledge to go out and come in before this people, for who can rule this Your people, that is so great?" (2 Chronicles 1:10).

God finds this request so satisfactory that He assures Solomon he will not only be given wisdom to govern the people, but also "wisdom and knowledge... riches, possessions, and honor, such as none of the kings had who were before you and none after you shall have the like" (2 Chronicles 1:12).

There are two things we can glean from this. First of all, the stories of our real God are so much better than the stories of genies in a bottle who limit you to three wishes. God is more like "Your request was so good, I'm gonna give you even more!" That cheapskate genie from Aladdin wouldn't even let him wish for more wishes.

But I digress. The second thing to learn here is that if God assured Solomon that he was wiser than any other king, it's worth seeing what Solomon wrote about it.

Describing this gift of God, Solomon explains, "It is He who gave me unerring knowledge of what exists, to know the structure of the world and the activity of the elements [...] for wisdom, the fashioner of all things, taught me" (Wisdom 7:17, 22). Beyond knowing facts, wisdom is described as understanding the "structure of the world" and — for the more poetically inclined — "a reflection of eternal light, a spotless mirror of the working of God, and an image of His goodness" (Wisdom 7:26).

Examining these passages, words like *fashion*, *structure*, and *working* stand out — explaining not just what is (the sky is blue; water is wet), but how we can understand that everything created is intended to give glory to God and help us to know Him better.

Wisdom is the gift of the Holy Spirit that enables us to take what we know about God — the "facts" of Christ, sin, and salvation — and apply it to the way we live our lives in the world. Wisdom helps us see what God intended for us when He created the world, and it helps us choose what will make us happy or fulfilled.

At any given point in the day, week, month, semester, or year, we have choices to make about what we do with our time and talents. All we do should be done with the final goal of heaven in mind. Sometimes this is easy. When faced with a choice to hug a small child or steal her candy, we know hugging will make us both happier and feel closer to God, while stealing is wrong. But what about the choices that are less obvious?

When I had the opportunity to attend work camp, I knew that this was one option of many for that week in the summer. Those were the facts. However, I also knew, on a level deeper than what a brochure could tell me, that there was a goodness to the community I would encounter and the actions we would do that week. I had learned this information from my friends and youth leaders, but it was the gift of wisdom working in my heart that helped guide my decision.

Wisdom helped me to see that while my choice to serve the needy at work camp for the week might not be as fun or easy as spending the week in the pool or at the beach, it was the choice that was mindful of what in the world would bring me closer to God.

Christ assured us, "If you continue in My word, you are truly My disciples, and you will know the truth and the truth will make you free" (John 8:31–32). Catholic writer Flannery O'Connor is said to have cleverly re-phrased this as "You shall know the truth, and the truth will make you odd."[1]

Seeing the world as God has ordered it and understanding that we exist for union with Him in heaven allows the truth to penetrate all the misconceptions we may see about what will really make us happy and holy — but as Flannery O'Connor supposedly explained, it also might make us a bit odd in the eyes of our friends and family.

For example, when I told my friends outside of youth group that I was going to work camp, they questioned that it would be a fun way to spend a week. "Cold showers? Cafeteria food? And you have to pay for this?" they inquired. I was sheepish before I left — it sounded silly when they put it that way. However, showing off the picture of the bathroom sink I built, they totally wished they had come, too. Actually they didn't — they still thought I was weird. But I knew that work camp had been one step in living the life God wanted for me, and it didn't really matter what my friends thought.

−ST. DAMIEN−

Just a few years ago, in 2009, Pope Benedict XVI canonized St. Damien de Veuster. Born in Belgium in 1840, he joined the Congregation of the Sacred Heart of Jesus in 1859. In 1864 he landed in Honolulu, Hawaii, as a missionary and was soon ordained a priest.[2]

---

[1] *Preaching and Teaching: Sermons by a Teacher Seeking to Proclaim the Gospel*, Ralph C. Wood, 2009). 135.
[2] *Libreria Editrice Vaticana.* (n.d.). *St Jozef Damien de Veuster (1840-1889).* Retrieved from http://www.vatican.va/ news_services/liturgy/saints/2009/ns_lit_doc_20091011_de-veuster_en.html.

You may remember from your history class that in the 19th century Hawaii had established a quarantined colony on the island of Molokai where all those suspected of having Hansen's disease (leprosy) were sent. These lepers were suffering and isolated from their friends and families, and the missionaries worried about the care of both their bodies and souls.

Knowing the risk of working among those with leprosy, St. Damien volunteered and served on Malokai for 16 years, dying of leprosy at the age of 49. When Pope Benedict XVI canonized St. Damien on October 11, 2009, he stated: "In order to follow Christ, Fr. Damien not only left his homeland but also risked his health: therefore... he received eternal life."[3]

I'm sure St. Damien's friends and family were doubtful that his decision to go to Malokai was wise — even the local bishop wouldn't force anyone to go "in the name of obedience" since everyone knew it was essentially a death sentence. St. Damien chose a life that made no sense if he was trying to climb the corporate ladder of worldly success or happiness, but he was unconcerned with these things. The life of St. Damien was a perfect example of how to be the "reflection of eternal light" that Solomon described as wisdom (see Wisdom 7:26). St. Damien wasn't seeking the approval of the world; instead he was trying to show the world God through his words and deeds.

St. Damien's life was so influential that I remember learning about him in social studies in third grade. I'm sure we talked about him in Sunday school eventually, but his decision to spend his life serving the people of Molokai inspired not just Catholics or Christians but the author of a secular third-grade social studies textbook.

We might not be called to serve the poor in a remote corner of the world, but the gift of wisdom in our lives can cause us to make choices that might seem odd to those who fail to see the bigger plan of God. Choosing to serve those in need instead of taking a summer vacation, choosing to serve in a parish ministry instead of being on a sports team or choosing to cook dinner for your family instead of taking a nap are all choices that might not be obvious to others, but following Christ has never been about the easy or obvious course of action. Wisdom helps us to see the world as God sees it; wisdom guides us as we seek to do His will.

----

[3]Libreria Editrice Vaticana.(11, October 2009). Homily of His Holiness Benedict XVI. Retrieved from http://www.vatican.va/holy_father/benedict_xvi/homilies/2009/documents/hf_ben-xvi_hom_20091011_canonizzazioni_en.html

How can you grow in wisdom and see the structure of the world as God intended?

- Find wise people and spend time with them, especially people who are older than you and have had years to reflect on the experiences you're currently having. Age doesn't instantly grant wisdom, but it does mean that one has had more experiences in life and has hopefully learned from them. Respect your elders and learn from them.

- Read about the lives of the saints — they offer us countless examples of lives aligned with the plan of God and not the logic of the world.

- When faced with a decision, reflect before you react. The loudest voices in your life might not be the wisest. Wisdom is found in prayerful reflection, not on the Internet.

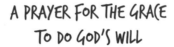

A PRAYER FOR THE GRACE TO DO GOD'S WILL

Grant me grace, O merciful God, to desire ardently all that is pleasing to Thee, to examine it prudently, to acknowledge it truthfully, and to accomplish it perfectly for the praise and glory of Thy name. Amen.[4]

---

[4]John O'Connell and Jex Martin, *The Prayer Book* (The Catholic Press, 1954), 91.

UNDERSTANDING

-REAL LIFE-

The first time I drove a car was when I was fifteen. My dad drove our family station wagon to the huge vacant lot of the local high school. If you've seen the movie *Vacation*, about the Griswold family vacation, you'd be amused to know that my real-life-Griswold parents owned a car very similar to the one Chevy Chase drove with his family to Wally-World.[5] Opening the door for me, my dad ushered me into the driver's seat and assumed his place as a passenger.

Now that I've been a passenger as my younger siblings learned how to drive, I know just how harrowing it is to turn the wheel over to an amateur. My dad, ever the un-fazed parent, simply suggested that I get used to the feel of steering a car by coasting around the parking lot in neutral. Bulking steel barge that it was, the station wagon cruised around the light poles at a breakneck seven miles per hour, and I marveled at how, unlike a video game or go-cart, I was driving a real car on a kind of real road with a very real passenger. It didn't seem that hard. Why in the world do you need to pass a test to get your license?

Believing I was ready for the next step, my parents enrolled me in driver's education with Coach Brown, the local athletic director who

---

[5]*Harold Ramis, director; Vacation, Warner Brothers, 1983.*

also taught the whole town to drive. When he pulled up in a taupe Honda Civic with the yellow "Student Driver" placard strapped to the roof, I was ready to try driving in first gear instead of neutral.

Gesturing in my direction, Coach Brown said, "You can drive to the parking lot." Drive to the parking lot? Up until that point, my experience had definitely only been driving in parking lots. The route to the lot he had in mind involved highways, stoplights, back roads and a tricky left-turn arrow. "Uh, I, uh, have only driven in neutral," I stammered. "Don't worry," he assured me. "I have a brake on my side, too."

As if a brake on his side was all that was necessary to prevent me from driving the taupe Honda and my friends contained inside to certain disaster.

My mom said that as I drove away, my friends in the backseat pressed their faces against the window and mouthed, "Help me!"

How supportive of them.

My hands were shaking and sweat was pouring down my back as I navigated the Honda to the highway. Creeping along at least 20 miles under the speed limit, Coach Brown assured me I was doing fine, but I was not convinced.

Stopped at an intersection, I panicked when my foot on the pedal didn't cause the car to accelerate. "Oh my gosh, I broke it!" I cried.

"No, you're just pressing the brake," Coach Brown calmly replied. "Try the other pedal."

Oh.

Gradually, I learned the ins and outs of driving beyond neutral gear. Signals, left-hand turns, merging into traffic, even blocking unsuspecting tourists on the inside lane of our beach-town traffic circles. After the required hours on the road, Coach Brown handed me my course certificate and wished me luck.

My first time driving solo to work, I still froze at an intersection, too afraid to venture across the highway to get to Walmart on my break. Sitting at the light, I realized that I *knew* what to do. I had practiced this dozens of times with Coach Brown and later with my mom and dad — who had finally allowed me to put the car in drive. The light cycled from red to green, and I boldly conquered the highway — and my fears.

I rocked the Griswold family station wagon for a few years in high school, borrowing it from my parents when I needed to get to church or work. Then I came home from my first year of college with a busier summer work schedule, and my parents thought we should acquire an extra car.

An old Saab was listed in the classifieds. Pulling into the owner's driveway, I immediately fell in love. It was from the late 80s, painted white with black details and a tan leather interior. I had never seen anything quite like it — it was nothing like the contemporary Honda Accords and Chevy Malibus my friends were driving. The Saab had a tape deck and an FM radio with buttons and knobs to operate it.

It was so hip.

"Oh, Dad," I gushed, "I could name it Sven, after it's homeland." (Saabs are manufactured in Sweden. Little did we know they were about as temperamental as the Ikea furniture you assemble in you dorm room that breaks as your first guest sits on it. I've never been to Sweden, but I can only assume its residents tread lightly around their cars and furniture.)

Sven, in addition to being very hip, was a standard transmission — a stick shift. My mom, who had grown up driving Volkswagon Beetles and Rabbits, assured me that I'd master this skill in no time. I was sure of it, too — watching my mom, whom I had never seen play a video game and needed help to play a tape in our VCR, deftly shift from first to second to third gear, I assumed it would be a cakewalk for me. I knew how to send emails and play Tetris, for crying out loud.

When I took the steering wheel for the first time, my mom explained that I needed to disengage the clutch while the car was in park. Then, I should shift to first gear while I gradually released the clutch and gave the car the gas. Oh, and I better practice on a flat road before I learned when to release the emergency break, to prevent Sven from rolling backwards.

Ok. Piece of cake. Engage clutch, first gear, gassssss-lurch. Sven, who had been so docile for my mother, suddenly buckled and threw us both back into our very hip, black seatbelts.

"Oh my gosh, did I kill Sven?" I asked.

My mom was laughing at me. "No, you just stalled out. That's what happens when the clutch doesn't engage."

Stalled out? But I had released the clutch and applied the gas just like my mom had done. "You have to find the sweet spot," she explained. "The exact moment that the gears are lined up — that's when you can accelerate and not stall. Right now you're popping the clutch and it's not engaging."

I was partially in awe (since when did my mom know such technicalities?) and partially overwhelmed, as I realized learning to drive a standard transmission might not be as easy as I thought.

Sven, while totes adorbs (totally adorable), proved to be an especially difficult transmission to master. I would later drive trucks and SUVs with very forgiving transmissions that rarely stalled. Sven was anything but forgiving. If the shift into first gear wasn't executed with exact precision, it would shudder and stall. I'd then have to restart the car, ignoring the angry drivers honking behind me. Barreling around town, I felt like everything Coach Brown had taught me about driving was no longer enough to even get me to the end of our driveway. I began to have nightmares about stalling out in inopportune places, like bridges and intersections.

I kept practicing, but I just couldn't finesse the right moment to accelerate and not stall. Stopped at a stop sign with my mom a few days later, I attempted to engage first gear a dozen times. Sven refused to budge. Mom, eying the cars backed up behind us, suggested that she take over. Humiliated, I traded places, Chinese fire drill-style, so she could drive us home.

The next week I stalled out in one of our cul-de-sacs. Inching my way across the circle, I just couldn't get Sven to stay in first gear long enough to get going. Neighborhood security approached in a patrol car, and I was mortified to see that the officer was Steve, the cutest guy on staff.

The patrol car slowed as he rolled his window down. "Everything OK?" he asked. "We got a call that someone was having trouble on this street." (Yes. My driving looked so bad that someone called and reported it.)

Cheerfully, my mom yelled from across the steering wheel, "Oh, she's fine, Steve. Just learning how to drive a stick shift."

"Ah," Steve nodded. "More gas, less clutch," he advised, chuckling a little to himself. He drove away, leaving me in angst while my mom giggled and said, "You girls are right. Steve is cute."

Finally, about three weeks after Sven had tormented both my waking and sleeping hours, I began to sense the right way to shift gears. I still stalled, but it was less frequent and I no longer had to call my mom to bail me out. I felt confident enough to drive Sven around town and even braved a few hills.

By the end of the summer, shifting gears was second nature. I was just as confident with a clutch as I had been with an automatic. I hadn't realized just how much more there could be to driving. Learning to shift gears had been hard work, but it would serve me well. Not only could I putter around town in my cute little Saab, I was never limited by what I could drive in the future. This came in handy when I lived in Central America, where most cars are not automatic.

—APPLICATION—

While it could be said that I first learned to drive when my dad set me loose in the parking lot to cruise around in neutral, the reality of my "drivers education" was that it unfolded over the course of several years. First I learned stopping and steering with my dad. Then Coach Brown set me loose on the open road where I learned how to navigate traffic and parallel park. Years later, Mom taught me the complexities of shifting gears and not stalling in front of cute security officers.

To this day, there are situations I encounter while driving that require extra thought and practice. I understood the basics at age 15 — gas to go, brakes to stop, and the steering wheel will move you to the left or right — but with each car I drive and each city I live in, I have to learn more about how to apply the basics of accelerating, braking and steering.

Through His words and deeds, God reveals Himself to us. We can look at the order of the world and see that there is a power greater than ourselves that created all we see. We can read Scripture and see that God sent His Son to show us how we are to live. We can look at the traditions of the Church, handed down to us from Christ, to see that He established His Church on the rock of St. Peter (see Matthew 16:18).

We are given a choice. We can either ignore these acts of God or we can believe. This act of belief, our response to God, is called faith. Faith is described by St. Thomas Aquinas in the *Catechism* as "an act of the intellect assenting to the divine truth by command of the will moved by God through grace" (*CCC* 155). That's a wordy explanation, but each word packs a punch when we break it down. Aquinas is explaining that it's our intellect — our brain — that can realize that there is a "divine truth." We observe the miracle of the world existing, the truth of Scripture and the existence of the Church to lead us to heaven, and we can see that there is an absolute truth that is divine — from God. It's grace that moves us to make the choice — or "command the will" — to say yes to God with our mind, heart and soul.

> "NOW FAITH IS THE ASSURANCE OF THINGS HOPED FOR, THE CONVICTION OF THINGS NOT SEEN. FOR BY IT THE MEN OF OLD RECEIVED DIVINE APPROVAL. BY FAITH WE UNDERSTAND THAT THE WORLD WAS CREATED BY THE WORD OF GOD, SO THAT WHAT IS SEEN WAS MADE OUT OF THINGS WHICH DO NOT APPEAR" (HEBREWS 11:1).

Faith is our response, our belief, in God. However, belief in God does not give us an instant and complete understanding and knowledge of all that He has taught us. Citing St. Anselm, the Catechism explains that "faith seeks understanding: it is intrinsic to faith that a believer desires to know better the One in whom he has put his faith and to understand better what He has revealed" (*CCC* 158).

This is where the gift of understanding works to help our faith. It is this gift of understanding that pushes us to go beyond acknowledging the existence of God (our belief) to figuring out His will for our lives — even when it's difficult.

When my dad took me to the parking lot, I could have sat behind the wheel and said, "Yep. This is a car. That's a road. But I'm just gonna chill out here and listen to the radio, because actually steering sounds kinda scary. I might make a mistake and hit something." Choosing to learn to drive a car is an intimidating step, but it's one that most of us will take because we have to do it if we're going to get to places on our own.

Just as I didn't master driving overnight, the gift of understanding is given to most of us gradually (for an example of this gift being given not so gradually, see the conversion of St. Paul in Acts 9). As part of the Second Vatican Council, the Church published a document on divine revelation. This document, *Dei Verbum*, explains that the Holy Spirit "constantly perfects faith by His gifts, so that Revelation may be more and more profoundly understood" (*CCC* 158). In learning to drive, I had my parents, classes with Coach Brown, the South Carolina Driver's Manual, and hours of practice to help me learn what I needed to know to get from point A to point B.

As we seek to live lives of faith, we can look to the many ways that God teaches us — through Scripture, tradition, the Church, our pastors, families, sponsors, and other role models of faith we may have — to help us grow in understanding.

When it comes to driving, my least favorite place in the entire world is Atlanta, Georgia. In just a few miles one will likely encounter twelve-lane freeways, funky intersections that branch out in six different directions, and hidden access roads. To make matters worse, every other road and establishment name involves the word "Peachtree." Directions to anything in Atlanta involves making a right onto Peachtree Road and then a left at Peachtree Highway and crossing over Peachtree Drive to arrive at Peachtree Mall, across from the Peachtree Commons. I'm not exaggerating — it's truly maddening.

Unfortunately, Atlanta is also home to some of my best friends and favorite shopping spots, so it's a city I frequent. I can still remember my first visit, when my friend Gayle gave me directions so I could make a coffee run. After she tossed me the keys to her car, I ventured onto the interstate. The 45 minutes that followed were some of the most harrowing in my life — I missed exits, I encountered intersections with crazy light patterns and I confused "Peachtree Drive" with "Peachtree Road." My teeth — and knuckles — were clenched the entire trip, but I eventually made it to Dunkin' Donuts and returned with our coffee and bagel sandwiches.

It was significantly more terrifying, but the same rules of driving that I had learned as a teenager worked on the Atlanta freeways. In the same way, the gift of understanding can carry us through both the serene moments of life — when having faith feels as easy as walking — and the moments when our feelings are in turmoil and we feel like we might lose our grip at any moment.

In the life and teachings of Christ, we see perfect understanding and a model of how this gift gives us a foothold when we feel the world has completely pulled the rug out from under us. The Gospel of Matthew describes how crowds began to follow Jesus as He was "preaching the gospel of the kingdom and healing every disease and every infirmity among the people" (Matthew 4:23). Stop and consider what this would have looked like — at a time when there wasn't even extra-strength Tylenol, Christ was being brought "those afflicted with various diseases and pains, demoniacs, epileptics, and paralytics and He healed them" (Matthew 4:24). When this man — who was making the blind see and the paralyzed walk — began to speak, people listened.

But what Christ said was new. In a day and age when riches and power were seen as favors from God, Christ taught us that it is the poor in spirit, those who mourn, the meek, those who hunger and thirst for righteousness, the merciful, the pure of heart, the peacemakers and even those who are persecuted and falsely accused who are blessed (see Matthew 5:3–11). Christ explained that He had come to fulfill the law of Moses — the Ten Commandments — teaching that while previously they had been told, "You shall not kill," Christ now said, "Every one who is angry with his brother shall be liable to judgment. Whoever says 'you fool!' shall be liable to the hell of fire" (Matthew 5: 22).

All through the Gospels, Christ brings love and truth to chaos — forgiving tax collectors, hanging out with prostitutes and ultimately asking pardon for the very people who would crucify Him. But don't think the life of Christ was a never-ending Hallmark special — Christ didn't hesitate to overturn the money changers' tables and make a whip to drive them out of the temple (see John 2:15–16). Christ, who is one with the Father and the Spirit, demonstrates perfect understanding and responds with truth, love and even stubbornness to reveal the Kingdom of God to the world.

-ST. THOMAS MORE-

The gift of understanding gives us the strength and perspective to see reality through the lens of eternity — not through immediate rewards or trials. We see this in the lives of the saints, and one of my favorite examples is St. Thomas More.

St. Thomas More was born in London in 1478. You probably remember from your history class that this period of time was like a real-life chessboard. There were kings, queens, knights, and bishops and no indoor plumbing. I imagine they spent a lot of time jousting, eating chicken legs, and drinking from goblets... but I might be getting this mixed up with the Renaissance Fair I went to in college.

St. Thomas More was a successful politician, and he was also a favorite of King Henry VIII. King Henry eventually appointed him to one of the most powerful offices in England: Lord Chancellor.[6] Throughout his political career, More's faith was his foundation; he led his family in daily prayer, Scripture study, and regular Mass attendance. Once, while More was at Sunday Mass, he was summoned by the king but he refused to answer him until Mass had finished.[7] (Something to keep in mind when you're tempted to check your text messages during the homily.)

The tension between his service to King Henry VIII and the King of the Universe would come to a head when the king sought a divorce from his wife of 17 years, Catherine of Aragon, so that he could marry Anne Boleyn. When King Henry asked (in that not-so-subtle way that kings request help) More to support this divorce and remarriage, St. Thomas More understood that "the key to the question was not in the obscure details of the marriage law but whether the king could dictate Church teaching and discipline."[8] In other words, St. Thomas More believed that the king did not have the power to tell the Church what to do.

Almost all of England — including most priests and all but one bishop — gave in to King Henry VIII and followed him as he established the Church of England, led by — you guessed it — the king of England. Parliament then passed the Act of Supremacy that "declared Henry as supreme head of the Church in England," and "it became a capital crime to deny that title. Every subject had to swear an oath affirming it, or face imprisonment."[9]

St. Thomas More chose imprisonment, refusing to lend his status to the king's shenanigans and arguing so eloquently at his London trial that the judge condemned him "without ruling on his objection"[10] — meaning his defense was so well crafted, it left the judge speechless. But this was never about giving St. Thomas More a chance to defend

---

[6]Thomas Paul Thigpen, Be Merry In God: Sixty Reflections from the Writings of St. Thomas More (Ann Arbor, MI: Charis Books, 1999), 12.
[7]Ibid., 13.
[8]Father Dominic Legge, O.P., "God's Servant First," Columbia, June 2012, 8–10.
[9]Ibid., 10
[10]Ibid., 10

himself and the Church; it was about getting him out of the king's way — either through changing More's mind or locking him up.

Throughout the ordeal, St. Thomas More never criticized the king — only eloquently defended truth and "took refuge in silence and prayer," trusting that God would give him the strength and courage for each trial he encountered.[11] When a messenger arrived at the Tower of London and announced, weeping, that More would be executed that day, More replied, "Be not discomforted, for I trust that we shall, once in heaven, see each other merrily, where we shall be sure to live and love together, in joyful bliss, eternally."[12]

After he climbed the scaffold where he would be executed, it was observed that More said little, only begging for prayers for himself and promising that he would pray for those present. Then, "he begged them earnestly that they would pray to God for the king, that God would give him good counsel, protesting that he died the king's good servant, and God's first."[13]

The gift of understanding helps us to place God above the world, above the pressure from friends, from teammates, from teachers, even from family. Understanding is the gift that enables us to navigate the world with eyes of faith and accept discomfort, suffering, sacrifice, and even — in the case of martyrs like St. Thomas More — death.

From the moment Christ began His public ministry, He pointed His followers to the reality of heaven and encouraged us to be "the light of the world" and "let your light so shine before men, that they may see your good works and give glory to your Father who is in heaven" (Matthew 5:16). The gift of understanding empowers us to live and work with heaven — not the world — as our home.

We don't learn to drive after one spin through a parking lot. In the same way, understanding happens gradually and takes practice. So how can you practice the gift of understanding in your own life?

----

[11]*Ibid., 10*
[12]*Legge, 10.*
[13]*Ibid.*

- Find wise people and spend time with them, especially people who are older than you and have had years to reflect on the experiences you're currently having. Age doesn't instantly grant wisdom, but it does mean that one has had more experiences in life and has hopefully learned from them. Respect your elders and learn from them.

- Get a copy of the *YouCat* or the *Catechism of the Catholic Church* and research your questions. These are authoritative resources for what the Church teaches, and they can help you grow in understanding. This is especially helpful for those moments when you know something is or isn't true but you're not completely sure why.

> FOR AN INSPIRING AND ENTERTAINING PORTRAYAL OF THE LIFE OF ST. THOMAS MORE, CHECK OUT THE PLAY *A MAN FOR ALL SEASONS* BY ROBERT BOLT, OR THE 1966 FILM ADAPTATION STARRING PAUL SCOFIELD.

- Be patient. Just like long division, English essays, and learning the scientific method takes practice, understanding our faith takes effort on our part. The difference between our faith and any other subject is that the heart of it isn't mere information — it's the person of Christ. It's okay to ask questions and struggle with tough topics. Seeking truth is, ultimately, seeking Christ.

- Spend time in prayer. Sometimes we can get so caught up in studying or thinking that we forget that it's the Holy Spirit that inspires our understanding. Don't hesitate to simply spend time in silence before Christ in the Blessed Sacrament. When you spend time in silence, you give the Holy Spirit the ability to get a word in. (Disclaimer: This works for questions of faith. Geometry proofs, on the other hand, are mastered through study.)

A PRAYER FOR UNDERSTANDING

O God, who givest light to every man, illumine us anew with an increase of faith and understanding. Cast out of our minds all unbecoming thoughts, all false and crooked reasonings. Banish from our hearts all pride and hardness and perverse desires. Bestow on us such protective grace that now harm may happen to our souls, that every ill may be turned to good, and our hearts be full of dutiful and holy love. Enable us to take up our cross daily and follow in the footsteps of our loving Savior, in fellowship with all Thy saints, whose prayers we beg, whose intercession we implore, through the same Lord and Savior Jesus Christ. Amen.[14]

[14] John O'Connell and Jex Martin, The Prayer Book (The Catholic Press, 1954), 97.

3

COUNSEL

—REAL LIFE—

In Advent, we often read from the prophet Isaiah who describes the Messiah as one who will have "a spirit of counsel" (Isaiah 11:2). For years when I heard this, I would think of my middle-school guidance counselor, Mrs. Hill.

Mrs. Hill was a meek woman who wore jewelry and vests with felt shapes sewn on that corresponded to upcoming holidays. She would show up in our classroom for "guidance counseling sessions" every so often and tell us that we were all really great and instruct us on how to tell each other the same. Mrs. Hill would direct us to write lists of compliments for each one of our classmates and have us draw pictures of our favorite things about ourselves. A visit to Mrs. Hill's office revealed posters with skydivers jumping in formation or puppies and cats having a tea party with the caption "Everything's Better With Teamwork."

From these experiences with a guidance counselor, I deduced that the gift of counsel must consist of giving compliments, spreading warm fuzzy feelings about teamwork, and maybe having a tea party with kittens.

The fall after I graduated from college, I lived in Belize, Central America, as a full-time volunteer at a Catholic mission. I say, "volunteer," but we did receive some compensation — room, board, and $12 a week. I knew that the "room" part of that equation would be pretty simple, but my four housemates and I were still a bit surprised when we were dropped off at a simple three-bedroom bungalow with a cement floor, five mattresses, and a table.

No chairs. No carpets. We had a sink, but no cups. There were lone fluorescent bulbs in each room that illuminated a whole lot of empty space. If we hadn't packed it in our suitcase, we would be living without it. It probably says a lot about my priorities that one of the first things I unpacked was a coffee maker. My roommate Cathleen unpacked her *InStyle* magazines. It wasn't like we were living in the Dark Ages — what did we need besides coffee and a fashion magazine? Still, there was a very important item that we soon realized we were lacking.

A mirror.

We didn't notice it until the next morning when we stumbled off our mattresses and rooted through our suitcases to find something presentable for our first day as teachers. Tugging on skirts and smoothing wrinkled T-shirts, we then scanned the wall out of habit, but there was no reflection to show us if our T-shirt was stained or if our skirts were fully zipped. Cathleen stepped into the kitchen — the open part of the room designated by the lone table that we were all standing around. For the most part, she was fine but her hair — usually one her best features — was parted weird. It was lopsided, like she had slept on it funny.

"How do I look?" she asked, the way girls ask when they are expecting to hear "Great!"

We looked at each other behind her back with some concern. We all knew her hair looked weird. Should we say something? We had to live with each other as roommates and colleagues for the next year — what if she took it the wrong way and got mad? How do you even tell someone that her hair looks weird?

Fortunately, the looks on our faces gave us away. "Is something wrong?" she said. "Well, " I began, "your hair..." I trailed off, unsure of how to phrase it and ruing the fact that had there been a mirror, she would have instantly noticed that she was having a bad hair day. Fortunately, Cathleen was never one to sugarcoat reality.

"Alison Griswold," she began (she always calls me by my full name when she thinks I'm not telling her the whole story, whether it's about a boy or a sale at the Gap that I'm trying to beat her to). Her eyes narrowed, and she placed her hands on her hips. "We do not have mirrors. We are about to stand in front of a room full of high schoolers. It is absolutely critical that you tell me how I look, and that you be completely honest."

"Your hair looks weird," I said bluntly. "I think you need to part it again and re-tie your scarf — it's lumpy over your left ear."

"Like this?" Cathleen asked, re-tying her scarf.

"Ahh, yes!" we all exclaimed.

Picking up her textbooks and water bottle, Cathleen walked out the door and began her first day as a high-school science teacher with un-lumpy hair, thanks to her roommates.

It was Cathleen who, a month later, took some of her paltry salary and bought the house a mirror from the Taiwanese grocery store on the corner. It was about a foot high, pastel green and had pandas on it with the words "how cute" and "smile time" lining the borders. Still, it was our only mirror, and it was given the place of honor on the table so that we could all take advantage of it.

Between the arrival of the mirror and that first day when I told Cathleen her hair looked weird, we quickly stopped worrying about offending each other and were brutally honest when asked the question, "How do I look?" Bad hair, wrinkled hems, sweat stains, mismatched shoes — we called it like we saw it. We were charitable, but we were honest because we knew that if we didn't help a sistah out, she'd look ridiculous in front of her whole classroom.

That month I learned two things. I learned how to apply mascara without a mirror (tip: don't sneeze). I also learned that sometimes other people see you better than you see yourself (especially if you don't have a mirror). I realized that Mrs. Hill wasn't a good example of "counsel" because she only taught us to give compliments and point out what was good. While this is really important, counsel goes beyond the warm fuzzies.

—APPLICATION—

In the Gospels we see Christ as the master counselor who did not need to rely on motivational posters or puppy dogs, because He possessed the spirit of counsel that Isaiah prophesized so many years before the Incarnation. One of my favorite examples of Christ as the master counselor is when He meets the woman at the well.

When Jesus was passing through Samaria, the Gospel of John tells us that He stopped to rest by Jacob's Well (see John 4:6). Getting water from the well, in the time of Christ, was like getting Froyo or organic coffee. It was a social experience. Women would go together to get water and chat it up, since texting hadn't been invented yet.

> INCARNATION "THE FACT THAT THE SON OF GOD ASSUMED A HUMAN NATURE IN ORDER TO ACCOMPLISH OUR SALVATION IN IT" (CATECHISM OF THE CATHOLIC CHURCH 461). BASICALLY THIS IS WHEN GOD BECAME MAN IN THE PERSON OF CHRIST.

That's why it's unusual that, while Jesus is resting, a woman approaches the well to get water all by herself. This was the Samaritan equivalent of sitting alone at the cafeteria table. Even though Jesus knows exactly who she is and what she's up to, and even though it was completely taboo for a man and a Jew to speak to a woman and Samaritan those days, He breaks every protocol and says, "Give me a drink" (John 4:7).

The woman calls Jesus out, asking, "How is it that you, a Jew, ask a drink of me, a woman of Samaria? For Jews have no dealings with Samaritans" (John 4:9). Jesus goes on to tell her, "If you knew the gift of God, and who it is that is saying to you, 'Give me a drink,' you would have asked Him and He would have given you living water" (John 4:10). The woman is intrigued by this living water — about which Jesus says, "Whoever drinks of the water that I shall give him will never thirst; the water that I shall give him will become in him a spring of water welling up to eternal life" (John 4:14).

However, when the woman asks for this water, Jesus tells her to go get her husband. The woman's statement, "I have no husband," seems irrelevant until we read Jesus' reply: "You are right in saying,

'I have no husband'; for you have had five husbands, and he whom you have now is not your husband" (John 4:18).

Had this been a middle-school guidance-counseling session with Mrs. Hill, I'm guessing she would have told Jesus that He needed to find something nicer to say about the woman at the well than pointing out her struggling love life. She might have told Jesus that He should have complimented the women about how good she was at finding so many husbands, or pulled out a puppy dog poster.

Fortunately for the woman at the well, this was Samaria and not my middle school, and Christ was in the business of sharing the truth — not compliments. When the woman states that she knows the Messiah is coming, who "will show us all things," Jesus states: "I who speak to you am He" (John 4:25–26).

After this revelation, we read that the woman literally left her water jar at the well and went to the very people she had initially distanced herself from, stating, "Come, see a man who told me all that I ever did. Can this be the Christ?" (John 4:25). As a result of sharing her encounter with Christ, "many Samaritans from that city believed in Him" (John 4:39).

The month I spent in a house with five girls and one small mirror, I learned that there are times when it is important to go beyond compliments and speak the truth — especially when your friend is about to walk out the door with weird-looking hair. However, this doesn't make it easy. That's when the gift of counsel comes to our aid.

When Cathleen asked me about her hair, at first all I could say was, "Uh," and that was just because I didn't want to critique her hair; it had nothing to do with her relationship with God, which is clearly of much greater importance. It is natural to not want to say things that our friends might find unpleasant, and this is where the gift of counsel empowers us and even helps us find the right words to speak.

I witnessed an incredible example of this from the now Blessed Teresa of Calcutta when I was 12 years old. My mom plopped my sisters and I in front of our television set and turned on the National Prayer Breakfast being held in Washington, D.C. My mother had the foresight to realize that this humble sister from India would be a saint one day, so she made us turn off the after-school cartoons and watch Mother Teresa address the leaders of the United States.

Rising to speak before President Clinton, First Lady Hillary Clinton, Vice President Al Gore and his wife Tipper — all outspoken supporters of legalized abortion — Mother Teresa was barely visible over the microphones on the lectern. Yet she addressed the most powerful leaders in the United States forcefully, declaring, "I feel the greatest destroyer of peace today is abortion because Jesus said if you receive a little child you receive Me. So every abortion is the denial of receiving Jesus. Is the neglect of receiving Jesus."[15] This was met with spontaneous, thunderous applause from the audience that lasted for over half a minute. Even with our very non-high-definition TV, though, I could see that the president, vice president and their wives were not applauding with the crowd.

THROUGH THE WONDERS OF TECHNOLOGY, YOU CAN WITNESS THE SAME SPEECH ON THE INTERNET: JUST SEARCH "MOTHER TERESA 1994 NATIONAL PRAYER BREAKFAST SPEECH."

At the time, I was intimidated at the idea of wearing a pro-life T-shirt in gym class. I believed abortion was wrong, but I was unnerved at the thought of sharing this unpopular belief. I can remember getting off the couch and moving closer to the television to be sure I was hearing her correctly. While it was common knowledge that Mother Teresa disagreed with the president about abortion, I was completely in awe that she would be so brazen. She was speaking the truth to a room full of some of the most powerful people that most publicly opposed it.

She didn't stop there, though. She continued, "Any country that accepts abortion is not teaching its people to love one another but to use any violence to protect what they want. This is why the greatest destroyer of love and peace is abortion."

More spontaneous applause. More discomfort.

It was awesome. That day, Mother Teresa was not concerned about what people thought about her or if she'd get invited back to breakfast with the president of the United States. All she cared about was sharing Christ through her words and deeds.

----

[15]C-Span. (1994, February 03). National Prayer Breakfast [News Broadcast]. Retrieved from http://www.c-spanvideo.org/program/54274-1.

Counsel is not about making people uncomfortable or embarrassed; it is the gift that empowers us to bring truth to light with our words and actions. Blessed Mother Teresa's confessor, Bishop Leo M. Maasburg, described her in the words she often used to describe herself. As "the pencil in the hand of God, in the hands of a God who was writing a love letter to the world."[16] As we strive to put this gift to use in our own lives, I find that analogy to be helpful.

When Christ spoke to the woman at the well, His goal was to show her the error of her sin and invite her to eternal life. With the gift of counsel, we are empowered to imitate Christ in this way. Our question before we act should be, "Am I being a pencil in the hands of God? Am I adding to His love letter? Or am I doing this because I know it will make me look cool or snarky?"

This is not an easy balance! That's why we need a supernatural gift to help us. So how can you practice the gift of counsel in your own life?

- Talk less, listen more. Christ asked the Samaritan woman questions He already knew the answer to, just so He could hear her explain. The gift of counsel helps us not just speak the truth but also patiently listen.

- If you are to speak the truth, you have to know the truth. Study your faith through reading Scripture, the *YouCat* or *Catechism* and apologetics resources.

- Don't make stuff up if you don't know what to say. Humbly admit that you're not sure what to say and then, if you have the opportunity, you can help find the answer.

---

[16]EWTN News. (30, August 2010). Mother Teresa's Confessor: She was 'a Pencil in the Hand of God'. Retrieved from http://www.ewtnnews.com/catholic-news/World.php?id=1529.

A PRAYER INSPIRED
BY ST. FRANCIS

Mother Teresa began her talk at the National Prayer Breakfast with a prayer inspired by the life of St. Francis. As we strive to use the gift of counsel to be "a pencil in the hand of God," it's a powerful meditation.

Lord, make me an instrument of Your peace.
Where there is hatred, let me sow love;
Where there is injury, pardon;
Where there is doubt, faith;
Where there is sadness, joy.

O divine Master, grant that I may not so much seek
to be consoled as to console,
To be understood as to understand,
To be loved as to love;
For it is in giving that we receive;
It is in pardoning that we are pardoned;
It is in dying to self that we are born to eternal life. Amen.

FORTITUDE

—REAL LIFE—

My friend Ali had one of the coolest bedroom set-ups you could have as a teenager: She had her own bathroom, her own TV, her own phone, *and her own entrance*. She and her sister shared a hallway that was on the ground floor of the house, and her parents and the rest of the living area were two or three floors above her. My parents did not realize that spending the night with Ali meant essentially zero adult supervision from the time I was dropped off to the time I was picked up.

In spite of all that freedom, sleepovers with Ali were low-key and consisted of me sneaking M&M's and pretzels into my sleeping bag (for all the freedom they gave her, Ali's parents stocked only very healthy, non-sleepover-friendly food in the kitchen) and watching *The Sound of Music* or *Annie* and talking about books all night. In the morning we'd walk out of her super-cool private entrance (which was technically a sliding-glass door, but in my mind it was in its own zip code) and go to the pool down the street.

Sleepovers with Ali were awesome.

For Ali's 12th birthday, Ali invited me and a couple of other friends to spend the night. I figured this was going to be another great night at Ali's, only better since birthdays meant a lift on the junk food embargo that usually surrounded her house.

Initially it was. There were a few friends that I already knew well and a few girls I hadn't met yet. We dove into the usual routine of junk food and movies. However, as the credits to *The King and I* began rolling, Beth — one of the girls I had just met — suggested that we start prank-calling boys.

At this point I should probably explain that phones used to be receivers with no screen that identified who was calling you. You actually had to speak up to identify yourself when you made a call by saying, "Hi, this is so-and-so. May I please speak to so-and-so?" For kicks, the youth of the nineties made "prank calls" — calling each other and instead of announcing their identity saying things like, "Hi, is your refrigerator running? Then you'd better go catch it!"

Between that and M.C. Hammer, it was a wild decade.

Instead of poking each other on Facebook, this was how we would awkwardly flirt. Beth got out our school directory and began prank-calling the boys, putting them on speakerphone. While I would have preferred we watched *Annie*, I tried to giggle along with the others. I wasn't too keen on talking to boys yet, but I knew this was what we were supposed to be into, so I tried to fit in. While the conversations began innocently enough with "Orange you glad I didn't say apple again?" it quickly drifted to some awkward boy-girl stuff involving baseball bases that I didn't understand.

Then, the boys on the other line suggested we go meet them on the beach.

Right then.

In the dark.

Without adults.

Beth looked at us all, expectedly. I had thought this was all talk, all a joke. I think Ali and my friends had, too, but the look on Beth's face showed that she was making this a dare for us all to keep up with her sophisticated understanding of middle-school socialization.

I felt a little sick. It was Ali's birthday, and I didn't want to be a party pooper. However, I had a pretty good feeling that Ali didn't want to go meet boys in the middle of the night. I knew that, like me, Ali would not even know what we were supposed to *do* with boys in the middle of the night, but my gut feeling was that it wasn't something I wanted to learn from Beth as an eleven-year-old.

"I'll call you right back," Beth said to the boy on the other line.

Turning to us, she asked, "Well?"

Everyone else looked down, avoiding her question. Popping some M&M's for courage, I finally squeaked, "I don't think that's a good idea."

Beth's eyes narrowed in my direction. While no one else had said they were down for a midnight rendezvous, I had just said I *wasn't*. She had clearly not expected this.

"Oh, I get it. You're religion won't let you," she sneered at me.

Religion? What did that have to do with anything? I just wanted to watch *Annie* and eat M&M's. What did this have to do with my religion?

"Uh. No. Uh...." I really didn't know what to say.

"Well, everyone else wants to," Beth said.

This, I was very sure, was untrue. However, my eleven-year-old brain was struggling to process all that was happening. In just a few minutes we had gone from eating junk food to talking to boys to this girl singling me out and picking on me for my religion. Looking back, I realize that Beth knew that if she could get me to agree to change my mind, everyone else would follow my lead, afraid that she'd pick on them, too. It's how bullies function. She probably sized up the cross on my neck and figured picking on me for being "religious" would be the quickest way to get me on board with her midnight escapade.

I did feel my friends silently leaning on me — knowing that they were too afraid to say anything but that they were going to follow me either way. If I said, "Aw, you're right. Let's go sneak out and meet boys on the beach. Let me go get Monopoly so we have something to do to pass the time," they would have followed Beth and I out the door.

But something in my head and heart knew that this would not be good. Were the boys "bad boys"? I have no idea. But the way they were talking about "second base" made me think they didn't just want to meet us for a softball tournament. With my friends still silently watching our standoff, I told Beth, "I, uh, just don't think we should."

Finally another girl murmured, "Yeah, me neither."

Furious that the tide had apparently turned against her, Beth stomped over and, after overturning the bowl of M&M's, shoved me to the ground. This was more for the theatrics since I was already sitting and she shoved me into a pile of pillows. Still, it was not a "friendly shove." She was ticked. She stormed into the bathroom and slammed the door and didn't speak to me for the rest of the night.

It was awkward.

We went back to eating M&M's and doing magazine quizzes. I didn't do anything more, like lead the group in prayer and tell them about Jesus or try to befriend Beth (I was honestly too afraid she'd shove me harder if I made eye contact with her again). I moved my sleeping bag a bit farther away from hers, and I was surprised to find myself shaking from the adrenaline of it all when we finally started to fall asleep. Sensing the tension, no one felt like going for a swim the next morning, opting to call their parents for early pick-ups. I went home feeling a bit weathered, but strangely content that I had stood up to Beth and spoken for my friends when they were intimidated.

Reflecting on that night, I wasn't really sure where the courage to stand up to Beth came from. She was bigger, clearly more knowledgeable about the ways of the world than I was and I wasn't the type of kid who enjoyed conflict.

—APPLICATION—

Fortitude is a gift of the spirit and a virtue that helps us stay the course when we find ourselves in situations like I did at Ali's sleepover. Sometimes we can anticipate a challenge or difficulty we'll face, like having to sit through an awkward family dinner or a difficult test at school. We can plan ahead — think of conversation topics and study — and show up prepared for what we think might happen.

However, there are times when we are totally unprepared for what the world throws at us. For example, a friend turns to you in homeroom and asks to look at your paper to get the answers for last night's homework. A teacher says something about Catholicism that you know is not true. Or, in my case, an innocent sleepover turns into a standoff. I wasn't expecting to have to do it, but I could feel this nudge in my heart moving me to stand up to Beth, even though my friends couldn't find the words to.

That nudge that kept me moving in the right direction? That was fortitude. That wasn't my own strength; it was the Holy Spirit giving me what I needed.

I realized for sure that it wasn't my own strength a couple days later. My mom had picked me up from school, and out of the blue she asked me if anything had gone wrong at Ali's birthday party.

"Uh. No. It was fine," I replied.

"Well," Mom continued, "I only ask because it was the strangest thing. In the middle of the night, I woke up and just felt so certain that I needed to pray for you. It was almost like a voice — maybe your guardian angel or something — whispering in my ear, telling me, 'Get out of bed and pray for Alison right now.'"

"Oh. Cool. Thanks," I mumbled.

"Well, I just wanted you to know that I did that. Do you want chicken or pork chops for dinner tonight?"

I was playing it cool, but inside, my head had exploded a little. I wasn't about to tell my mom what had happened, but I was amazed to realize that she was praying for me by name, in the middle of the night. I was even more amazed that she had done it at a moment that had been especially difficult.

We've all received the gift of fortitude through the Sacrament of Baptism, and it is strengthened when we are Confirmed. There are also people in our lives who are praying for us to be courageous and steadfast when it's difficult, just like my mom prayed for me.

Fortitude can be a scary gift to use, though. The *Catechism* tells us that it's the virtue that "ensures firmness in difficulties and constancy in the pursuit of the good" (*CCC* 1808). Did you catch the "firmness in difficulties" part? This means we won't grow in fortitude in our struggle to finish a piece of chocolate cake or an all-night *Hunger Games* marathon. That's pursuing *fun*. That's easy.

We grow in fortitude when we take the steps to do what we know is right, even when it's not easy or popular, even when people make fun of us or think we look ridiculous. Fortitude is what helps us focus on what God wants for us instead of what's going on around us. Think of it as headphones that tune out every message you're hearing except for the Word of God, whispering in your heart and leading you to do the right thing.

You may feel alone when you step out, but with your Catholic family you're in great company. Our faith is full of examples of young saints who tuned everything out but God and did things that some would consider crazy or even impossible. For example, St. Dominic Savio, who, as a student, stopped his friends from fighting by holding a crucifix between them while declaring that they could throw the first stones at him. St. Maria Gorretti was brutally murdered at the age of 14 but died forgiving her attacker.

What these saints had — and what you have — is the promise of Christ: "In the world you have tribulation; but be of good cheer, I have overcome the world" (John 16:33). No matter how difficult, unexpected, unnerving, or scary a situation may be, we can be confident that Christ conquered the world and is awaiting us in heaven.

We can know this in our heads, but acting on it can be much harder. So how do you act with fortitude? How do you practice using this gift in your own life?

- Pray! All the saints in heaven are praying for you (what the Church calls the "Communion of Saints") but don't forget to pray every day for the Holy Spirit to show you what to do when you're not sure.

- Read about saints who were courageous when faced with difficult choices and think of them when you're wondering what you should do.

- Keep trying — you may mess up. You may not know what to do sometimes. That doesn't mean that you don't have the gift of fortitude; it just means you're human. Even St. Peter denied Jesus three times under pressure from the crowd.

A PRAYER FOR FORTITUDE

Lord, when I am faced with a difficult choice or an unexpected challenge, grant me the courage to conquer fear and uncertainty and do what You would want. Amen.

5

KNOWLEDGE

-REAL LIFE-

When I was a kid, I really wanted to be a computer programmer. Then I learned that job involves more than just playing Tetris all day. Never mind, then. Next I wanted to be a teacher. This aspiration actually stuck, and I looked for chances to teach the young'uns as soon as I hit middle school and had a height advantage going for me. My little sisters were the first victims, as I tried to help them with schoolwork and teach them what I knew. This didn't last long; they were better students than I was.

Babysitting held some better opportunities to practice my future career since these kids were significantly younger, and unlike my sisters, they didn't know I had a C-minus average in English. As soon as I turned 11, I signed up for the American Red Cross Babysitting Course and learned important things like how to dial 911 (hint: it's exactly what you'd think) and making sure you had a way to contact parents in case of an emergency. That isn't as obvious as it sounds, because there were no cell phones back then. Babysitting meant receiving an itinerary for the evening and paging restaurants when dogs wouldn't stop barking or kids wouldn't stop crying — or bleeding, for that matter.

With my American Red Cross Certification nestled in my wallet next to the punch card I was working on to earn a free Personal Pan

Pizza from Pizza Hut, I was ready to take on the neighborhood. The calls rolled in, too. I had a reputation for not allowing too much television when kids were awake and not talking to boys on the phone while the kids were asleep (which was easy because talking to boys meant actually knowing boys to talk to). I really did enjoy improving my teacher skills while babysitting; I would try out craft projects and have kids sound out words during story time. I could even read a book and show the pictures at the same time. No waiting to see illustrations when I was reading on the couch, no sir.

One of my favorite kiddos to babysit for was a little girl named Lisa. She was a sharp three-year-old who enjoyed getting quizzed on her ABCs, learning new words and drawing elaborate pictures of her family on big easels. Occasionally we'd break for tea parties.

Lisa's mom, Joan, noticed my enthusiasm for the preschool crowd and approached me with a question — and an offer.

Joan was a member of the local synagogue and the coordinator for their children's programs. They were searching for someone who could do lessons for Lisa and her preschool classmates while the adults met for prayer. "I've found a great textbook for them to use," Joan explained. "It's actually for Catholic Sunday Schools, but I love how they tell the Bible stories." Showing me the books, she explained that I'd have a class of five little ones for about an hour a week. I'd be able to tell them stories from the Bible, do crafts, and teach them prayers.

I was ecstatic at the thought. To be so young and already be courted as a teacher was so flattering! I would be the coolest teacher these preschoolers had ever encountered, a cross between those well-dressed teachers you see on Nickelodeon shows, with all sorts of cool facts and examples, and Maria Von Trapp from *The Sound of Music*. I could lead songs on the guitar I would learn to play and perhaps even sew uniforms out of curtains.

"Of course, you'd have to take out the references to Jesus," Joan added, interrupting my daydream.

"Huh?" I said, bringing my daydreams back to the kitchen counter and the preschool religion textbook open between us.

"Well, we don't believe in Jesus," Joan explained. "I mean, we don't believe Jesus was the Messiah. So you'd have to stick with the Old

Testament when you planned your lessons. Teach whatever you'd like from the Old Testament, just don't bring up Jesus."

Oh. "Can I get back to you?" I asked her.

"Sure — I hope you can do it," Joan said, reassuringly. "You're so good with Lisa, and of course we'll pay you."

My cool-teacher-meets-Maria VonTrapp fantasy resumed, only now I was hitting the mall with extra cash to spend on trendy accessories at Claire's Boutique, thanks to my sweet synagogue-teaching gig. Maybe I could finally get a second hole pierced in each ear or jeans from the Gap. Or maybe I'd be able to afford lotion and shower gel from Bath and Body Works (at $9.50 a bottle, my friends and I only seemed to have enough cash left for one or the other when we went shopping). Teaching the Bible for cash — what could be better?

The only thought that nagged me, as I pedaled home, was the condition Joan had placed on the whole experience.

You'd have to take out the references to Jesus...

It wasn't like I'd be *lying* to the kids. I'd be teaching them all about the Old Testament. That's like more than half the Bible. It's like five-sixths, if you want to get technical. I wouldn't be lying to the kids; I just wouldn't be telling them the whole story. If I were teaching Sunday School at my own church, I'd even be using the same book. Only this would be even better than my own church, because I'd be teaching the Bible and getting paid! My church didn't do that, that's for sure.

But you couldn't tell them about Jesus.

Grrr, why wouldn't that funny feeling in my stomach go away? Maybe I needed to eat something or take a nap. This was a great offer, a chance to practice teaching kids about God. A chance to make money. There was nothing about this that wasn't awesome.

Which is what I excitedly told my mom when I arrived home. How I had the chance to be a teacher, to have a classroom, to use a teacher's manual, and *get paid*.

She listened and then asked dubiously, "Do they know you're Catholic?"

"Uh-huh, but Miss Joan said I'm so good with Lisa, she thought I'd be the best for the job."

To her credit, Mom didn't point out that, at 12 years old, I'd also be an affordable option. She just listened patiently as I shared everything Joan had told me.

"So you'll use a Catholic Sunday School book?" she asked. "You'd certainly know your way around that. But wouldn't there be an awful lot in there about Jesus? Do they want you to teach their kids that you've found the Messiah they're still waiting for?"

> LIKE MANY STORIES IN THE OLD TESTAMENT, THE STORY OF ABRAHAM AND ISAAC (FOUND IN GENESIS 22) IS A FORESHADOWING OF THE NEW TESTAMENT STORY OF GOD THE FATHER SACRIFICING HIS SON FOR US. SAINT AUGUSTINE ONCE SAID, "THE NEW TESTAMENT LIES HIDDEN IN THE OLD, AND THE OLD IS UNVEILED IN THE NEW."

"Well," I began. How had I convinced myself that this wouldn't be a problem? Oh right — I'd be teaching them the Old Testament. Over half the Bible. "Miss Joan said that I'd teach them the Old Testament parts." I pulled the textbook out of my backpack (the *teacher's manual*, I might add) and showed it to her. I opened it up to the chapter on Abraham and Isaac. "Abraham and Isaac," I said. "Just like what I learned in Sunday School when I was their age."

Mom pulled the teacher's manual over to her side of the table. Flipping to the next page, she pointed to a picture of Jesus on the cross. "And how would you explain this to the little Jewish preschoolers?" she asked.

The book was comparing Isaac to Jesus. Why didn't I see that coming?

"Well, I guess, uh, well, I guess I wouldn't be able to."

Saying it out loud, that funny feeling in my stomach came back.

Gently my mom continued, "You are a good teacher. And I don't think this is the last chance in your life that you'll get to teach. But I think you should pray about this. Do you really think you can teach God without teaching Jesus?"

She continued, "Look up Matthew 10:32. This is your decision, but I think you should read that verse first."

I went to my room and dug my Bible out from one of the stacks of books and sketch pads that were balanced all over my desk, chairs, and floor.

Finding the Gospel of Matthew, I turned to chapter 10. Christ was sending His disciples out to share the kingdom of heaven, assuring them that they shouldn't be afraid. I found the passage my mom had pointed me to:

> *"So everyone who acknowledges Me before men, I also will acknowledge before My Father who is in heaven; but whoever denies Me before men, I also will deny them before My Father who is in heaven"* (Matthew 10:32–33).

This was pretty black-and-white. No matter how I tried to rationalize it, the reality of teaching at the synagogue was that I might have to either disobey my instructions and answer the kids' questions about Jesus or deny Him. Granted, it'd be denying Christ to a bunch of preschoolers, but it would still be denying Him.

My *Sound of Music*-meets-cool-teacher daydream was replaced with another. Only this one was much less pleasant. I had recently learned about *The Last Judgment* by Michelangelo, which depicts Christ sending people to heaven or hell. I had always put myself in the category of someone that would be sent to heaven. But here, spelled out, Christ was telling me that teaching at the synagogue could place me in the category of people He turned His back on when the time came.

Yikes. What had I been thinking? I suddenly felt very, very aware of just how not OK it would be for me to accept Miss Joan's invitation.

Briefly, I contemplated being a renegade teacher — taking the job and then sneaking lessons about Jesus into the classroom when no one was watching. However, it wouldn't be very honest of me to accept a job and then deceive the parents of young children. That didn't seem like the best way to introduce these nice Jewish people to followers of the Messiah. They probably got enough sneaky evangelization, living in the Bible Belt.

No, it was best to be honest. I told Miss Joan I didn't think I was the right person for this job, but I thanked her for thinking of me.

I still babysat for Lisa. We still read books, practiced letters, and had tea parties. And the next time I saw *The Last Judgment*, I did so with a renewed awareness of the fact that, at some point, I too would face Christ and be judged. I might not know everything about Christ, but I knew He was the Messiah. And while I might not be carrying a sign saying "Let me tell you about Jesus" up and down Main Street, I'd better not deny knowing who He was, either.

A few years later, when I was a freshman in high school, our church opened a parochial school. They had a few students in the prekindergarten class who were still adjusting to English as their second language. The teacher, Miss Rose, approached me about helping this little group for a few hours a week.

It wasn't my own classroom. I didn't get a teacher's manual or a paycheck. However, during the hours I spent each week with preschoolers, I felt like I was on my way to being a real teacher, and it was awesome.

There's one moment that especially stands out in my mind. By December, I had been volunteering for a few months and the preschool teacher and her aide must have felt confident enough to leave me unattended for a few minutes while they ran an errand down the hall. They asked if I minded watching the class for a minute.

Did I mind? A classroom to teach! This was the moment I had been waiting for! My mind began racing with what I could teach them in, well, the minute or so I would have.

"Do you want Miss Alison to tell you all a story?" Miss Rose asked.

"Yeah!" they replied. Eighteen little munchkins sat around me, their legs crisscrossed underneath them on the carpet circle.

A story it would be. But which one?

Duh. Jesus.

"Do you guys want to hear a story about the most important person ever?" I asked them.

"Yeah!" they exclaimed. Well, that's a relief. Note to self: Don't ask preschoolers a question if you don't have a backup plan.

"Well," I explained, "I'm going to need some help. First, I need some students who can play little sleeping animals."

Arranging the student volunteers at the head of the class, I explained that they were the sleepy animals in the stable. We took a vote and decided there was a sleeping cow, a sleeping pig, and a sleeping goldfish. (The viability of a fish in a stable with no water was for another lesson.)

Next I asked for some volunteers to be shepherds and little lambs. Placing them far away from the stable, I explained they had taken the lambs far away so they could find grass to eat. They were all really tired, so they were all sleeping in the grass they had found.

Eighteen little preschoolers were totally transfixed on the story unfolding on their carpet square.

"Now, I need two people to be very important parts of this story. I need a Mary and a Joseph."

Taking my volunteers by the hand, I led them to the door of the classroom. "How do you get to school in the morning?" I asked them.

"My mom's van," the little Mary answered.

"Right," I explained. "Everyone here gets to school in a car, right?"

"Yes," they chorused.

"Well," I continued, "Mary and Joseph didn't have a car or a van. They had a donkey, so Joseph let Mary ride it. They walked for many, many miles to get to our little stable here. Imagine how tired they are! But here they are, at the stable."

(I opted to skip the "no room at the inn" part. If I pulled an innkeeper from the class, I might run out of kids before I got to the angel chorus which would be a total buzz-kill).

"This was the only place they could find to stay," I explained. "All the hotels were booked, so they had to sleep next to the cow and the pig and the goldfish. Are you all cozy now?"

The ensemble in the stable nodded and made very loud snoring noises.

"In the middle of the night, do you know who was born?"

"Jesus!" they all yelled. It was a Catholic school, after all. They weren't hearing this story for the first time, but I could tell they were using their imaginations to see it in a new way.

"That's right!" I said. "And Jesus was so important that God wanted the shepherds to know about it right away. When God has a message, He sends an angel. Everyone still sitting down, you all get to be angels! Who are you going to give a message to?"

"The shepherds!"

"That's right!" I said. "And you're going to tell them a big announcement! You're gong to say, 'Glory to God in the highest, and peace to His people on earth!'"

Even if the angels didn't quite get the words right, they definitely out-did me in enthusiasm. "Glory to God! Peace! Highest people!" — or something like that came from my angel chorus.

At that point I looked up and saw Miss Rose and her assistant watching from the doorway, smiling. I realized it had been more than a minute, but they had let me keep teaching.

"So," I explained, "that was what happened the night that Jesus, the most important person ever, was born. He was the most important person ever because He was sent by God to show us how much God loves us. Who here is friends with Jesus?"

Eighteen hands shot into the air. "Let's say a prayer and thank God for sending us Jesus," I said.

We finished with a prayer, and Miss Rose took over again, but not before whispering, "You did a great job with that!" to me.

As preschool lessons go, it was short — and it may have led a few of them to believe that goldfish sleep in stables. However, those few minutes of teaching the prekindergarten class at St. Francis Catholic School about Jesus, I felt — and forgive me for being a little dramatic here — that I was doing what I had been created to do. I wasn't just teaching the kids some facts or telling them a story — I was sharing Christ with them.

I didn't know everything about Jesus (I still don't), but as I arranged those kids in the classroom and told them the story of Jesus, I took everything I had been taught about Jesus, everything I loved about being a Catholic Christian and everything that inspired me about the reality of God becoming man in the person of Christ and shared it with the 18 little ones in my charge.

As great as extra mall money from the synagogue would have been, I can honestly say that the joy I felt teaching the story of the birth of Christ to those little preschoolers far surpassed the happiness that could come from any accessory sale at Claire's. Because it wasn't just the kids that were learning. As I was explaining the story of Jesus, even though I had heard it a million times, I felt like I was getting a new appreciation for my faith from their wonder as I shared.

-APPLICATION-

Knowledge as a gift of the Holy Spirit used to make me very nervous, because if my grades in school were any indication, it was a gift I thought I totally lacked. While I was fortunate to have wonderful teachers, I found school pretty hard and really had to work at studying. To this day, I'm in awe of people that can memorize information on a page they've only glanced at, regurgitate facts they've heard once or do math in their head without scratch paper. From middle school all the way to college, my academic victories were limited to the areas of reading and writing. Every other subject was such a struggle that during my last year of high school, I seriously considered not going to college.

Did my less-than-stellar grades mean that somehow the Holy Spirit had forgotten to give me the gift of knowledge? For a while I really thought so.

Still, I remembered the morning in that prekindergarten classroom. I had taught those kids something. I didn't think my meager grasp of the Gospels was lofty enough to be called "knowledge," but something had happened there. It dawned on me that maybe knowledge as a gift of the Holy Spirit and knowledge measured by the SATs were not the same thing.

In the first letter of St. Paul to Timothy, he explains that God "desires all men to be saved and come to the knowledge of the truth. For there is one God, and there is one mediator between God and men, the man Christ Jesus" (1 Timothy 2:4–5). The gift of knowledge — the gift from the Holy Spirit — isn't "book smarts." It's knowledge of the truth, which St. Paul explains is *actually* a relationship with a person.

The difference between the gift of knowledge and the knowledge that helps you pass your algebra test is that you don't have a relationship with algebra. Algebra exists as something to help you understand and order the world, but algebra does not have strong feelings about you, your happiness, or your eternal future. Pass or fail it, and algebra will still just be staring smugly from your textbook, daring you to solve the x in "$10 = 4x - 2$." Don't confuse your teacher pursuing your homework with algebra pursuing you. It's not.

Christ pursues. Christ is not a subject; He's not material to be mastered or a test to be passed. Yes, we will all face judgment one day, but don't think of it as a final exam. Rather, it's a moment that St. Paul describes as "the surpassing worth of knowing Christ Jesus my Lord." He explains that he "suffered the loss of all things, and count them as refuse, in order that I may gain Christ and be found in Him" (Philippians 3:8–9). It's the gift of knowledge that guides us into this relationship that allows us to begin to see Christ as our Savior, and in turn, realize that we are *found* in Him.

This is why that moment in the prekindergarten class was a transformative moment for me. In sharing Christ with the little munchkins, I wasn't sharing mere information; I was sharing a *person*. In the same way, this is why I got sick to my stomach when Miss Joan invited me to teach the preschoolers at the synagogue about the Old Testament, but not about Jesus. The gift of knowledge moves us to grow in relationship with Christ and then share Him with others. To teach about God and not Jesus would have meant denying this relationship.

Consider what we know from other relationships in our lives: It's great when we meet a new friend from school, church, or band camp. You bond while studying and eating mystery meat in the cafeteria, or playing messy games and talking about the Bible or whatever it is you do at band camp. You text, talk, and maybe even get matching best-friend key chains. One day, at Walmart, you see your friend with her mom. You approach them, say "Hi," and introductions happen.

In a human relationship, we might not know everything *about* each other. I met one of my best friends, Gayle, in college. Having grown up in different parts of the country for the previous 19 years, there was a lot about each other that we didn't *know*. After years of friendship, there are still things we don't know about each other even though we talk almost every day. I don't know what she had for dinner last night; she doesn't know that I once had a green belt in karate. Still, we would never say that because we don't know everything about each other, we don't *know* each other, because having a relationship with someone means constantly growing in knowledge.

Think back to the scenario I described — where you meet your new friend with her mom in Walmart. What if, instead of introducing you to her mom, your friend suddenly became awkwardly quiet and didn't return your friendly greeting? What if they turned around and ignored you? Maybe you've experienced this in a relationship already — it goes far beyond awkward; it stings to be rejected by someone we thought we knew and loved. A healthy relationship is about pursuing knowledge of the other person.

The spiritual gift of knowledge nourishes the relationship that is our faith. Just like we want to *know* about our family and friends because we care about them — and the more we know, the more we tend to care — the gift of knowledge causes us to want to know more about and be known by the person of Christ.

The *Catechism* echoes the words of St. Paul, explaining that "whoever is called 'to teach Christ' must first seek 'the surpassing worth of knowing Christ Jesus'" (*CCC* 428) and then explaining that "from this loving knowledge of Christ springs the desire to proclaim Him, to 'evangelize,' and to lead others to the 'yes' of faith in Jesus Christ. But at the same time the need to know this faith better makes itself felt" (*CCC* 429). This is the work of the Holy Spirit in our lives — making our need to both know and share Christ felt.

-ST. CATHERINE OF SIENA-

Born in Siena in 1347, St. Catherine grew up in an affluent family as the youngest of 25 children (yes, you read that correctly: 25). Feisty from a young age, she was determined to spend her life in service to God, despite initial opposition from her family who wanted her to marry. She even went as far as to cut off her hair to deter potential suitors.

Her family finally conceded to her desires and allowed her to become a Dominican tertiary.

When she was 19, she was praying in her room and "the Savior appeared to her, accompanied by His blessed Mother and a crowd of the heavenly host. Taking the girl's hand, our Lady held it up to her Son who placed a ring upon it and espoused Catherine to Himself, bidding her to be of good courage, for she was now armed with faith to overcome the assaults of the enemy."[17]

Catherine gained a following of people who were attracted to her love and service to the poor, the sick, and the imprisoned. Many also began to seek her advice and counsel and were inspired by her words to reform their lives. She even became known as a mediator and was sought after to settle disagreements between businesses and cities.

Catherine's counsel didn't stop at the local level. In 1305, Pope Clement V made the decision to move the papacy (the office of the pope) from Italy to Avignon, France, in an effort to escape the warring families of Italy and live in greater comfort.[18] For 70 years the popes (while still maintaining an unbroken line of succession from St. Peter) led the Catholic Church not from Rome, Italy, but from Avignon. Sent by the town of Siena to Avignon to mediate political disputes, Catherine took up the cause of not just peacemaker but of convincing Pope Gregory XI that he needed to return the papacy to Rome.

> A TERTIARY IS A LAYPERSON (SOMEONE WHO ISN'T A PRIEST OR A SISTER) WHO HAS MADE VOWS TO A RELIGIOUS ORDER (LIKE THE FRANCISCANS, DOMINICANS OR CARMELITES) WHO PRAYS FOR AND PARTICIPATES IN THE GOOD WORKS OF THE COMMUNITY WITHOUT NECESSARILY WEARING THE HABIT OR LIVING IN COMMUNITY.

While "the greatest men of the age" had attempted to convince the popes to return to Rome, it was Catherine who convinced Pope Gregory XI to act "without loss of time," and he returned to Rome in 1376. Both Pope Gregory XI and his successor, Pope Urban VI,

---

[17]Michael Walsh, editor, Butler's Lives of the Saints (Brewster, Massachusetts: 2005), 125.
[18]Alan Schreck, The Compact History of the Catholic Church, Revised Edition (Cincinnati: Servant Books, 2009), 63–64.

would continue to seek the advice and counsel of St. Catherine until she died at the age of 33.

When she wasn't advising popes, Catherine dictated a book, *The Dialogue of St. Catherine*. Why dictation, you ask? This woman, known for her instruction and ability to exhort political and religious leaders, never learned to read or write. Not only was St. Catherine canonized in 1461, she was declared a Doctor of the Church — a saint whose teachings are seen as especially useful — in 1970 by Pope Paul VI.

> THERE ARE 34 DOCTORS OF THE CHURCH, AND FOUR ARE WOMEN: ST. TERESA OF AVILA, ST. THÉRÈSE OF LISIEUX, ST. CATHERINE OF SIENA, AND MOST RECENTLY, ST. HILDEGARD OF BINGEN.

St. Catherine of Siena's knowledge of God wasn't the result of academic study but of prayer and her ardent desire to deepen her relationship with God. She simply explained that "everything comes from love, all is ordained for the salvation of man, God does nothing without this goal in mind" (*CCC* 313). Her knowledge was a relationship with God, whom she loved.

This isn't to say that you should take the St. Catherine of Siena approach to knowledge and forgo reading and writing while you await inspiration. St. Catherine took advantage of spiritual direction to help her grow in knowledge, as well as the ability to have secretaries to read and write for her.

So how can you grow in the gift of knowledge in your own life?

- Pursue Christ as you'd pursue any other relationship — with an investment of your time. Just as your relationships with friends and family will suffer if you don't spend time with them, your relationship with Christ needs an investment of your time. Commit to Mass attendance, the Sacrament of Reconciliation, and daily prayer.

- If you encounter experiences that you feel will confuse or undermine your relationship with Christ, leave them. This isn't being close-minded; this is guarding the most important relationship in your life. You wouldn't hang out with people who gossiped or trash-talked about your best friend. Why would you go to a movie, read a book, or spend time with people intent on undermining your relationship with Christ?

- When you encounter questions or feel confused, remember that not knowing everything about someone doesn't mean you don't have a relationship — it just means you need to ask questions and learn more. Don't hesitate to ask your parents, pastor, youth minister or Confirmation sponsor for help when you want to know more.

A PRAYER TO MARY

O Mary, Mother of fair love, of fear, of knowledge, and of holy hope, by whose loving care and intercession many, otherwise poor in intellect, have wonderfully advanced in knowledge and holiness, thee do I choose as the guide and patroness of my studies; and I humbly implore, through the deep tenderness of thy maternal love, and especially through that eternal wisdom who deigned to take from thee our flesh and who gifted thee beyond all the saints with heavenly light, that thou woudst obtain for me by thy intercession the grace of the Holy Spirit that I may be able to grasp with strong intellect, retain in memory, proclaim by word and deed, and teach others all things which bring honor to thee and to thy Son, and which for me and for others are salutary for eternal life. Amen.[19]

—St. Thomas Aquinas

[19] John O'Connell and Jex Martin, *The Prayer Book* (The Catholic Press, 1954), 107.

6

PIETY

Although I babysat for several years, by the time I was 14 my friends had started getting "real jobs," and I was eager to join this exclusive club of people who went shopping on "payday," complained about their bosses and ran around the house ironing uniforms and scarfing down their breakfast when they had to be at work by 11 on a Saturday morning.

My bike could take me to two options in a shopping center a few miles from home. Idyllically labeled "Main Street," this little strip had a grocery store and an ice-cream parlor. The grocery store was the standard option for many — they hired lots of local teens to bag and cashier. My friend Kelsey had just started working there and shared that the greatest stress was memorizing all the codes for produce. She showed me the list they had sent her home with — columns of numbers next to obscure fruits and vegetables.

"You have to know all of this?" I asked, incredulously.

"By heart," Kelsey replied, solemnly. "It's hard, because cucumbers and zucchini looks a lot alike. And I keep getting my apples mixed up."

I was impressed. Cucumbers and zucchini looked exactly alike to me, and I wanted nothing to do with lists of numbers. The grocery store was out, so I set my sights on the ice-cream parlor nearby, Sweet Sensations.

Sweet Sensations was an honest-to-goodness ice-cream parlor. Not Froyo, not gelato, not dippin' dots, or whatever else you all are into these days. This shop had a counter with stools, a jukebox in the corner and a little bell that jingled when the door opened and shut. Booths lined the walls, and there was a Pac-Man game that took quarters. It was owned and managed by a couple of die-hard Yankee fans who found themselves in the South and took it upon themselves to decorate the walls in homage to their favorite baseball team in the midst of Braves country.

The challenge was that, unlike the grocery store, Sweet Sensations only hired a few people and you had to be able to carry drinks on a tray and make a curlicue shape when serving soft-serve ice cream. I reasoned that while people had to go to the grocery store, they got ice cream when they were happy, and I wagered that working where happy people went would be way more fun. I filled out my first-ever application and was delighted when the owners, Bill and Sharon, called and invited me to come to talk to them.

What do you wear to an ice-cream parlor interview? I was full of angst, wanting to appear earnest and professional but realizing I also needed short sleeves in case they asked me to reach into the freezers and show them how fast I could prepare a sugar cone with Cookies and Cream.

When I arrived, Bill immediately launched into an explanation of the menu, the flavors, the specials board and how to make milkshakes without getting sprayed across the front of your shirt with the residue that would spew from the old-fashioned machine. Sharon showed me where I could request days off, where the schedule was posted (an index card in the kitchen) and she explained that I could keep the tips I made on tables but that the tip jar was divided up at the end of every shift. Milkshakes, schedules, days off, tip jars. My head was spinning.

"Can you come back tomorrow to train from 2:00–4:00 p.m.?" Sharon asked.

Was this my interview? No five-year plan? No questions about what animal I most related to or why I felt drawn to the field of dairy-based hospitality? The thought of all those numbers I could be memorizing at the grocery store jolted me back to reality.

"Uh, sure," I stammered.

"Here's your T-shirt. You can wear khaki shorts or jeans. No jean shorts or khaki pants. We'll make you a nametag if you get through your training this week."

And just like that, I was launched into the service industry.

Even though I didn't have to memorize produce codes like my friend Kelsey did at the grocery store, working at Sweet Sensations wasn't as easy as I thought it would be. There were endless combinations of sundaes to learn, trays to balance and we had to add our checks on a calculator like cavemen without computers.

Bill and Sharon were pretty nice, but they ran a tight ship and were quick to correct me, the new kid, when I was taking too long to make a milkshake or put in the wrong order for someone's lunch. I was eager to get it right, and I would feel frustrated when they'd just walk away and not give me a chance to explain that the chocolate ice cream was hard as a rock that day and was taking forever to scoop — or that the customer whose order I had messed up had also changed their mind 12 times and I had forgotten to cross out choice number 11 before dropping the check in the kitchen.

Then there were the customers. Some of them were really nice and would even slip me a dollar when I got the sprinkles evenly distributed on their kid's sugar cone. Others were terrible. They'd grumble, complain about things completely out of my control, like prices or flavors, and leave huge messes with no tip.

The whole experience was a lot to take in, and after about a month and a half I had mixed feelings about this whole job situation. Fortunately, I was going to a Steubenville conference with my youth group and would be taking a much-needed break from my new grown-up, job-related worries.

My youth group and I arrived at the conference, and they passed out the schedules. It looked pretty interesting, with lots of talks and music. However, I rolled my eyes when I saw "Holy Hour" on the schedule for Saturday night. A Holy Hour? This isn't what I had driven 12 hours to Ohio for. It wasn't that I was opposed to Adoration — but a whole hour seemed excessive. Fine for moms and grandmas, but there was no way I could concentrate that whole time. I wondered if I could possibly sneak back to the room for a nap when the time came.

The weekend sped by, and before I had time to devise an escape, Saturday night's Holy Hour arrived. There had been a lot of praying that weekend, but as we gathered in the tent, the speaker explained that this would be a special encounter with Christ and that we should pray for Him to touch us and heal us. We should reach out to God, our Father, and ask Him for whatever we felt we needed right then and there.

As the priest holding the monstrance entered and began to process toward the altar, I wasn't really sure what to expect. I was thinking about all the things I had learned that weekend, but I was also thinking about how working at Sweet Sensations for the last couple weeks had been my first encounter with "real-world" stress and the disapproval of others. Up until that point, I had only answered to my parents and teachers and Little League soccer coach — people who really cared about me, who affirmed me constantly and wanted me to succeed (even my soccer coach, which was nice of him because I was pretty bad at soccer). Being corrected by Bill and Sharon or yelled at by cranky customers made me realize that the days of being simply accepted as a kid were over. I realized that the world could be a kind of cruel place, full of people who would actually yell at a 14-year-old girl and watch her cry just because their milkshake was lumpy.

ADORATION: PRAYING IN THE PRESENCE OF THE HOST THAT THE PRIEST HAS CONSECRATED AT MASS THAT, BY THE POWER OF GOD, HAS BECOME THE BODY OF CHRIST. BECAUSE THE CONSECRATED HOST IS JESUS, IT IS A UNIQUE OPPORTUNITY TO BE IN THE PRESENCE OF CHRIST. (CHECK YOUR LOCAL CHURCH — THERE MAY BE ADORATION THERE!

Then the monstrance was placed on the altar and, staring up at Jesus, I knew in an instant that even if I kept messing up when I made change from the register and kept getting the Butter Pecan and Black Walnut flavors mixed up, even if I got fired and never made it in the sundae-making world, I was loved. Not for what I could do or what I had to offer the world — simply loved.

It wasn't like God spelled this all out to me — I didn't hear Him say anything or get a vision of Him parting a sea of Rocky Road ice cream. It was just a peace that I hadn't felt since I had begun working and had started worrying about all my inadequacies.

Kneeling with my youth group, I realized that it didn't matter if my new bosses thought I wasn't learning fast enough or if the customers were mean. God was my Father, and He loved me unconditionally.

Scooping ice cream would not be the last time I had these feelings. High school would include geometry proofs I never got right, unrequited crushes, the part in *The Sound of Music* that went to someone else and an inability to conjugate verbs in Spanish. Don't get me wrong — I didn't skip through these failures unaffected. There was many a night when I could be found sobbing over my Spanish textbook, completely confounded by the difference between *ser* and *estar*. But when I took a few deep breaths and my initial frustration died down, I knew God was there — and His love didn't depend on my skills; it was just there.

-APPLICATION-

When I hear the word *piety*, what comes to mind is the ladies in the front row of the church who pray the rosary before Mass. The way my grandmother always has her prayer book on hand. Priests walking around the garden, meditating on deep spiritual thoughts with their heads bowed.

In other words, I thought it was for church ladies, grandmothers, and priests. In my mind, to be pious or to practice piety meant being hunched over a prayer book, mumbling prayers in Latin with your hands folded and your eyes scrunched shut. Not that there's anything wrong with that. When it comes to prayer, Latin and prayer books have their place. But piety goes beyond posture.

It was an email from a high-school friend that helped me understand what piety looks like for the average Joe. Or Jane. Or in this case, Rachel.

Rachel spent a couple of years as a missionary in China, and because this was back in 2005, she used old-fashioned e-mail to update friends and family about what she was up to and what we could pray for. In her first e-mail update after arriving, she wrote, "Dad has been so faithful in taking care of me... I was able to find a tutor that will help me start learning the language." I read this and was really confused. I had just seen her father at Walmart a few days ago. I didn't think he had flown with her to China.

The next paragraph began, "One thing for you to intercede on my behalf to Dad for is the cold. The high these days is in the mid-teens, and the nights are very cold." Intercede on her behalf... like pray? Pray to Dad? In a face-palm moment, I realized *Duh! She was talking about her* heavenly Father. About God.

Rachel referred to God as "Dad." Initially, I admit, I was uncomfortable reading it. It seemed so casual. So trusting. It felt like one of those awkward moments when, let's say, you're grocery shopping with your mom and you turn the corner and your mom runs into someone she hasn't seen in years, and they launch into this deep conversation about mutual friends and feelings and someone who's had their gallbladder removed, and you're left standing there going, "Oh, soup's on sale. So that's cool." The more I thought about it, though, the more I realized that Rachel calling God "Dad" wasn't too casual or too intimate. I wasn't uncomfortable. I was inspired by what I now realize was piety.

God is our Father. God is our Dad. Piety is the gift of the Holy Spirit that enables us to see this.

The reason we struggle to embrace this as simply as Rachel did is not because of the "God" part, but because of the "Father" or "Dad" part. At some point, no matter how idealistic your life may be, you've probably clashed with your earthly father. Our earthly fathers are human; they're going to make mistakes or be misunderstood by us. Maybe you felt your curfew was unfair. Your dad didn't like your boyfriend or girlfriend. He wasn't open to your idea that you give up on eleventh grade (specifically geometry) so you could learn to play guitar and be the next singer-songwriter success story.

Maybe your story is more serious and your earthly father is either not in the picture for some reason or he has really hurt you through his words or deeds. For you, the word "father" doesn't conjure up positive memories or feelings.

The *Catechism of the Catholic Church* explains, "The divine fatherhood is the source of human fatherhood" (*CCC* 2214). Read that carefully. God is the first father, and our earthly fathers are supposed to imitate *Him*. However, because our earthly father is the first one we meet or at least hear about in real life, we can get it mixed up. We think of God as having the same imperfections as our father instead of being the perfect Father he's striving to *imitate*.

Or maybe you've felt the sting of disapproval from superiors or complete strangers like I did when I started my first job, and it left you feeling crummy, like you've failed to earn or deserve God's fatherhood.

When Jesus was 12, He traveled with His parents to Jerusalem for the Passover. The Gospel of Luke tells us, "When the feast was ended, as they [Mary and Joseph] were returning, the boy Jesus stayed behind in Jerusalem. His parents did not know it, but supposed Him to be in the company" (Luke 2:43–44). While most parents would notice, these days, if they had left a child behind on vacation, in the time of Christ people traveled in big groups, and the children would roam among their friends and family (probably searching for the donkey packed with the best snacks). We see that when Mary and Joseph realized that Jesus wasn't there, "they sought Him among their kinsfolk and acquaintances" (Luke 2:44). "Kinsfolk" would imply that this was a roaming family reunion — you know how easy it is to get lost in the shuffle when there are aunts, uncles, and cousins all tag-teaming the supervision.

Mary and Joseph returned to Jerusalem, where St. Luke tells us they spent three days searching. Finally "they found Him in the temple, sitting among the teachers, listening to them and asking them questions; and all who heard Him were amazed at His understanding and His answers" (Luke 2:46–47).

At this point, Mary asks a question with what appears to be a lot more composure than my mother would have demonstrated if I had decided to take a detour on the way home from our family vacation when I was 12. St. Luke tells us that Mary asks, "Son, why have You treated us so? Behold, Your father and I have been looking for You anxiously" (Luke 2:28).

Jesus replies, "How is it that you sought Me? Did you not know that I must be in My Father's house?" (Luke 2:49). The *Catechism* describes this moment when Christ explains that He is in His Father's house as revealing the prayer "which the Father awaits from His children [...] lived out by the only Son in His humanity, with and for men" (*CCC* 2599).

My experience with the gift of piety, of encountering God as my unconditionally loving Father, happened when I was in His presence. Even though it was a Steubenville conference with thousands of teens, Christ's presence in the Eucharist on the altar before me gave me a chance to "be in my Father's house." Piety is the gift of the Holy Spirit that moves us to seek our Father — not when we feel we've earned it, but when we are most in need of it.

How can you practice the gift of piety in your own life?

- Honor your father and mother. This is not always easy, but remember that your parents were given a special grace at your Baptism to mirror the love of God to you. This is not always easy, but seek out ways to honor your parents as a way to connect with the authority God has placed in your life.

- If your relationship with one or both of your parents is strained, talk to an adult you trust (pastor, youth minister, grandparent, aunt, uncle, counselor) for some objectivity about how this could affect your relationship with your Father in heaven. Good counsel can help strained relationships.

- Spend time in your Father's house. If spending time in church or in Adoration is difficult because of where you live, carve out time in your day for personal prayer wherever you may be — your bedroom, the kitchen table, the closet — and practice placing yourself in the presence of God. Allow Him to love you, His child, for who you are — not for what you do.

 THE PRAYER THAT JESUS TAUGHT

God is your Father. Your Dad. When the disciples asked Jesus how to pray, He instructed them to say:

Our Father who art in heaven, Hallowed be Thy name. Thy kingdom come; Thy will be done on earth, as it is in heaven. Give us this day our daily bread, and forgive us our trespasses, as we forgive those who trespass against us. And lead us not into temptation, but deliver us from evil.

Start there.

FEAR OF THE LORD

—REAL LIFE—

Melissa was a cool youth leader. Only 33, she seemed closer in age to us than the rest of the adults that would pack us into vans for camps and conferences. She knew the words to "Mmmbop," drank Mountain Dew instead of coffee and wore overalls. (Don't judge. That was the zenith of fashion in 1998.) She was teaching herself guitar and had learned the chords to "Shout to the Lord," her favorite worship song. She talked to us like we were her peers. We loved all our youth leaders, but we really loved Melissa.

One weekend on retreat we all found ourselves cooped up in the girl's dormitory, the afternoon's events postponed until a severe weather system passed by. Rain pelting against the windows, and the conversation meandered into different ways to pray. "I journal," Melissa explained. "Sometimes I don't even write things down — I just sketch pictures. Like this one."

Pulling out her journal, she flipped to a page that showed a little figure surrounded by dark, angry, swirly clouds. "This is what I drew the day I was diagnosed with cancer. I felt overwhelmed and worried about my husband and daughter — this picture was how I felt."

"Cancer?" we asked, alarmed. "You have cancer?"

"I did, but I've been in remission for years, goofballs." Turning to another page, she explained, "This was the picture I drew when I found out the treatments were working. I was so excited for my hair to start growing back!" She showed us a page of flowers and birds flying around, the words "Rejoice in the Lord, Always" scripted across them.

Reassured that Melissa was now healthy, the dark cloud that had temporarily hovered over our conversation passed, and we started giggling about which boys on retreat we thought were cute.

About a year later, Melissa's participation trailed off, and she didn't return that fall. We thought nothing of it, figuring her daughter had just needed extra help with homework that semester or something. We were pleasantly oblivious to the notion that anything really bad happens to people we actually know. I know I was, anyway.

I missed a youth group meeting on a weekend that my family went out of town. Keep in mind that this was before cell phones or texting, so I didn't actually get the news until I saw my friend Danielle at work later that week.

"Melissa came by youth group last Sunday," she told me while I rushed to put on my apron behind the counter at the ice-cream shop.

"Oh?" I asked, suddenly realizing it was the first any of us had heard from her all semester.

"She was wearing a scarf. She lost her hair again." Danielle said, her chin twitching a little to keep from getting emotional in front of the children sitting at the counter, happily eating their ice-cream cones.

My stomach felt queasy. If she lost her hair again, then that meant something bad. Something *really* bad.

"She has cancer again?" I whispered. Danielle nodded. "It's worse this time," she said.

Peddling home on my bicycle later that day, I felt like the little figure in the middle of Melissa's journal illustration, with dark clouds swirling around my head and everything I thought I knew about the world. Cancer was something that happened to older people, to great-grandparents and great-aunts and uncles who had passed away before I could really remember knowing them. Melissa was so cool. She was so nice to us.

She was so, so young to have such a terrible disease.

The whole situation felt terribly unfair. I knew that what I was feeling was no different from what countless others felt every day when they heard similar news about people they loved, but knowing that a disease like cancer existed was one thing. Knowing someone that was dying from it was a much harder reality to swallow.

When it became clear that Melissa was too sick to return to another youth ministry meeting, our leaders gave us her address and suggested that we send her our thoughts and prayers. I don't remember what I wrote to her, but she wrote back to me:

> I am very much ready to go to God when He calls, and my husband and daughter are ready to let me go (Praise to Christ Jesus!). Just when we think it is time, the Lord has chosen to give me a few more clear, happy weeks. He must have a purpose because I know His timing is perfect. I can't believe how good God is to me.

This seemed like such a different person from the woman who just a year before, had been chugging Mountain Dew and teasing us about our crushes. Just a year ago it seemed like Melissa was barely older than us teens — just a few steps ahead in life than we were, with decades left to go. Not someone measuring her time in weeks.

Just like Melissa had shown us an intimate look at her relationship with God when she first opened her journal, this note reassured me that she was continuing to trust God, that even her imminent death wasn't shaking her confidence that God is good.

A few weeks later, the phone rang. My dad answered and said, "I'm so sorry. OK, I'll tell her. You'll let us know when the funeral will be?" Hearing "funeral," I felt sick. Dad didn't even have to tell me that Melissa had passed away — who else would there be a funeral for?

I went to my room and lay on my bed. Melissa had been confident in the goodness of God. Confident that He had a plan. So fearless. I wanted to be, too. Yet God had just allowed something to happen that I didn't fully understand, something that seemed unfair and that was making me feel like I had a rock in my stomach and a knot in my throat.

−APPLICATION−

I'm afraid of lots of things. Snakes, heights, food on a stick, roller coasters, docks without railings, spiders — did I mention snakes and heights? I'm the lamest theme park attendee ever. Just watching people get on roller coasters makes me feel light-headed.

A few years ago I brought my youth group to a camp in Charlotte, North Carolina. We spent our free day at Carowinds, an amusement park that has some pretty sweet roller coasters. Unwilling to accept my "No thank you" to their invitations, I was finally pressured by the adults and teens to go on one of the smallest roller coasters in the park. Seriously, it was so puny that there wasn't even a height limit.

Sitting on the bench (this coaster was so wimpy it didn't even require harnesses), I could feel myself start to perspire. My hands clenched the safety bar, and I squeezed my eyes closed and began screaming.

"Miss Alison, they're just moving the car to load the next one. The ride hasn't started yet," the teens said, hushing me.

Oh.

Then the ride began in earnest, clunking its way up and down the track, careening through the air. We whipped back and forth on the bench where we sat, centrifugal force pushing us to one side and then to the other. The worst were the drops — when the car would slow down and creep up to the top point of a track. Hovering at the apex, the sky was all you could see if you looked straight ahead. Then the car would plummet toward the ground, leaving your stomach several feet behind.

As if all this wasn't torturous enough, the ride went around the track twice.

I hated every second. I could never let go of the fear that the cart would run off the track. That I would fall out. That somehow my final moments of life would be on this dumb roller coaster, before I had even gotten a chance to eat an elephant ear.

If you die on a roller coaster at church camp, are you a martyr? I digress.

The youth group was convinced that if they could just get me on one ride, I'd be converted and want to harness myself into the crazy Batman-Meets-Superman-and-You-Hang-from-Your-Feet-and-Hurl-through-the-Atmosphere ride.

Not a chance.

"Miss Alison, wasn't that fun?"

Wobbling off the ride, I struggled to fix my hair, clothing, and brain. It all felt permanently scrambled. Knees knocking, the park gradually stopped spinning around me.

"No. No, it was not fun. You guys are all crazy. And I will hold your bags for the next ride."

And that's what I did. I was much happier sitting on the rocking chairs, holding everyone's bags and water bottles, reading a book, and waiting to follow them to the next gate. Thrilling, I know. But that's what my fear of roller coasters means. I can't get past the overwhelming sense of pending catastrophe and just enjoy the thrill.

My fear of roller coasters could be seen as sort of silly. I haven't done the research (partly because I wouldn't trust it), but there are probably very few roller-coaster-related deaths reported each year. I've never actually seen anyone suffer any injury at the hands of an amusement park ride, and the one or two times I've been talked into trying a ride for myself, I've escaped, emotionally traumatized but unscathed. Even though I tell myself all these things, I remain unmoved and unconvinced that I don't put myself at a huge risk when I board a coaster.

While this makes me a great gal to hold the bags of the folks riding, I acknowledge that this fear also makes me kind of a buzz-kill to have around. I miss out on the shared experiences of "that crazy part where the track curls your socks inside out" or "when you sorta leave your seat flying down the mountainside."

Because of this fear, I miss out because I think that something might happen which most likely won't. This fear keeps me from experiencing things that might actually be fun for me.

Consider the list I shared earlier. With the exception of snakes — which can be poisonous or capable of strangling someone — there's not much traction to the logic of my other fears. I mean, food on a stick? Really? Don't ask me to explain. It's just so scary they way it could fall off and land in your lap or on your shoes at any moment.

With the idea that, in many cases, fear is something we should try to overcome, it can be a bit puzzling to read Isaiah's prophesy that the Messiah's "delight shall be in the fear of the Lord" (Isaiah 11:3). What does this mean? That the Lord is like a roller coaster or a poisonous snake?

Our language is limited, especially when we attempt to describe the work of God in our lives. However, rather than think of our personal experiences of fear like spiders, public speaking or clowns, it can be helpful to consider some of the times we see fear in Scripture.

At the Annunciation, when the angel Gabriel appears to Mary, he assures her, "Do not be afraid, Mary, for you have found favor with God" (Luke 1:30). Later, when the angels announce the birth of Christ to the shepherds, we read that "the glory of the Lord shone around them, and they were filled with fear" (Luke 2:9).

Then, after calling His disciples to follow Him and beginning His public ministry, we see that Christ takes Peter and James and John to a mountain where He is "transfigured before them, and His face shone like the sun, and His garments became white as light" (Matthew 17:2). Because there were no vampire romance novels written yet, the disciples would have been genuinely alarmed at this sight. And then they witness the appearance of Moses and Elijah and Jesus speaking with them (see Matthew 17:4).

I tend to minimize how truly alarming the sight of angels or Moses and Elijah must have been to Mary, the shepherds and the disciples — after all, weren't we just reading about them a couple pages back in the Old Testament? It's kind of like going to the Hall of Presidents and thinking that Washington and Lincoln probably went bowling together. We forget that they were not actually contemporaries; Washington was our nation's first president back in 1789 and Lincoln didn't take office until 1861.

Hundreds and hundreds of years separated Jesus, Elijah, and Moses. Angels — while we read about them frequently in Scripture — were no more commonly seen in Biblical times than they are in the local Walmart. In all of these moments in Scripture, God is making Himself known in a new way, and the response is fear. Not an "Oh my gosh, that snake might be poisonous so let me get my garden hoe" fear or a "No matter how many roller coasters you drag me on I still find them terrifying" fear, but awe that God is making Himself known in a way that we didn't expect and don't fully understand.

The *Catechism* defines the fear of the Lord as the gift of the Holy Spirit "which ensures our awe and reverence before God" (*CCC* 1813). In an age where we can Google, search Wikipedia or watch YouTube for almost any piece of information we want to learn more about, the ways of the Lord can remain difficult for us to fully understand. No book, website, app, or teacher could help me fully grasp why God allowed Melissa to die so quickly or so young. Even today, thinking about it gives me a feeling somewhat similar to the dread I feel on a roller coaster. The difference, though, is that while I still don't — and probably never will — trust roller coasters, I can be confident in God's plan and stand in awe of it... even when it includes suffering for me and those I love.

-BLESSED CHIARA "LUCE" BADANO-

Born in Italy only a few decades ago, in 1971, Chiara always demonstrated kindness as a young child, but she had a deep conversion at the age of nine. She described it as the moment that she "discovered the Gospel." She said, "I was not an authentic Christian because I did not live it completely. Now I want to make this magnificent book the sole purpose of my life."[20] She became very involved with Focolare, a movement of youth and families in the Catholic Church in Italy, and she tried to be an example to her friends and, in her words, giving Jesus to them "by the way I listen to them, by the way I dress, and above all, by the way I love them."

When Chiara was only seventeen, she experienced a pain in her shoulder while playing tennis. She discovered that she had osteogenic sarcoma — a serious and painful form of cancer. She would suffer for two years — losing the use of her legs along with her hair. With each trial, her offering was "For You, Jesus, if You want it, I want it too!"[21] To everyone — her family, her physicians, fellow patients and friends — she was a light of joy and consolation even while she was in tremendous pain.

Writing to her friends, she said, "Previously I felt another world was awaiting me and the most I could do was to let go. Instead I now feel

---

[20]*Focolare Movement. (n.d.). Adolescense. Retrieved from http://www.chiaraluce.org/page/adolescenza.*
[21]*Focolare Movement. (n.d.). Sickness. Retrieved from http://www.chiaraluce.org/page/malattia*

enfolded in a marvelous plan of God which is slowly being unveiled to me."[22] After two years of heroic suffering, Blessed Chiara died on October 7, 1990. Her last words to her mother were, "Good-bye. Be happy because I'm happy."

The day after her beatification, Pope Benedict XVI described her as "a ray of light" and "an example of Christian devotion" who shows us that the love of God is "stronger than evil and death" and credited the intercession of the Virgin Mary with leading youth "through difficulty and suffering, to love Jesus and discover the beauty of life."[23]

The life of Blessed Chiara contained suffering, uncertainty and even fear of the future and of the unknown ways that God was working in her life. However, rather than shying away from the difficulty that the future held, Blessed Chiara embraced it all with acceptance. She even refused morphine (to ease her pain), explaining that "it reduces my lucidity, and there's only one thing I can do now: to offer my suffering to Jesus because I want to share as much as possible in His suffering on the cross."[24]

The pain Chiara first felt in her shoulder. The moment Melissa learned her cancer had returned. The Angel Gabriel appearing to Mary. Shepherds witnessing a chorus of angels in the middle of the night. Elijah and Moses appearing with a transfigured Christ. These are all moments that must have begun with a certain element of real fear. The gift of the Holy Spirit, however, doesn't leave us feeling anxious or unloved. Soothing uncertainty with the reality that God's plan for us extends beyond our limited sight of the here and now, the gift of the fear of the Lord fills us with reverence and awe for God's power, confident that He is working for our good when we don't fully understand it.

This doesn't happen overnight. I didn't waltz into Melissa's funeral with a halo and serenity, assuring my friends that this was all part of God's plan for our lives. We cried. We missed her. We went to Taco Bell afterwards because it seemed like something that would make us feel better (a promise Taco Bell, of all things, can never deliver on).

---

[22]Focolare Movement. (n.d.). Departure. Retrieved from http://www.chiaraluce.org/page/partenza.
[23]Pope Benedict XVI. (2010, September 26). Angelus. Retrieved from http://www.vatican.va/holy_father/benedict_xvi/angelus/2010/documents/hf_ben-xvi_ang_20100926_en.html.
[24]Focolare Movement. (n.d.). Sickness. Retrieved from http://www.chiaraluce.org/page/malattia.

We were sad. And that's OK, because the Holy Spirit isn't limited by our feelings. He can work when we're joyful, sad, or experiencing any of the many other feelings we feel in a day.

What we did do is try to sing really loud whenever they played Melissa's favorite song, "Shout to the Lord," because the chorus described what we knew she believed and what we were learning. Hands raised, we'd belt out the words. We knew that's what Melissa would do if she were there, and while we were sad she wasn't with us anymore, the Holy Spirit gave us comfort and confidence in God's promise to her and to us.

How can you nurture the fear of the Lord in your own life?

- Countless artists have portrayed God's majesty over the years. Spend time meditating on the different images of God in art; the perspectives of others can give you a deeper sense of awe about who He is in your own life.

- If you experience fear or anxiety that keeps you from doing something you want to do, talk to a trusted adult — a parent, pastor, or youth minister. Sometimes you can be overwhelmed by all you see, and someone else's perspective can help you understand if your fears are helping you avoid harm or preventing you from something positive.

- Push yourself. I was afraid of roller coasters. I tried it and I still hated it. However, there are many other experiences that I was once afraid of — like riding my bike without training wheels, camping or moving to a new town — that weren't so scary after all. If it's something that could make you holier, happier and healthier, give it a try.

Draw strength and inspiration from the prayer of our Blessed Mother. At a time when she was very uncertain about what the future held, as an unmarried teenager, she prayed her Magnificat:

My soul magnifies the Lord, and my spirit rejoices in God my savior, for He has regarded the low estate of His handmaiden. For behold, henceforth, all generations will call me blessed; for He who is mighty has done great things for me, and holy is His name. And His mercy is on those who fear Him, from generation to generation. He has shown the strength of His arm, He has scattered the proud in the imagination of their hearts. He has put down the mighty from their thrones, and exalted those of low degree. He has filled the hungry with good things, and the rich He has sent empty away. He has helped His servant Israel, in remembrance of His mercy, as He spoke to our fathers, to Abraham and to His posterity forever.
— Luke 1:46–55

CONCLUSION

"The Holy Spirit comes into our hearts so that we as children of God might know our Father in heaven. Moved by God's Spirit, we can change the face of the earth" (YouCat, 113).

Does that statement give you chills? It should.

Re-read that passage from the *YouCat* and notice what it does *not say.* It does not say "With God looking on indifferently, we can change the world with our own strength." It does not say, "Moved by God's Spirit, we can give it our best shot." Nor does it say, "Give the Holy Spirit a try and see how it works out for you. You can always try something else if it doesn't work out."

The previous chapters shared the ways that I've experienced the gifts of the Holy Spirit, along with some ways the Holy Spirit was at work in the lives of the saints and holy people. However, if these examples didn't jive with you, or you're feeling lost as to what this means, be confident in this: The Holy Spirit empowers us by doing things in our lives that we cannot do on our own. Things that change the face of the earth.

–ST. PETER–

An excellent example of someone doing through the Holy Spirit what he could not do on his own is St. Peter. We think of St. Peter as the first pope and heaven's bouncer at the pearly gates, but we forget that his walk with Christ had a "rocky start" (no pun intended).

Let's visit a day, recorded in the Gospel of Matthew, when Peter was not yet Peter but Simon. Jesus is walking by the Sea of Galilee. "He saw two brothers, Simon who is called Peter and Andrew his brother, casting a net into the sea; for they were fishermen. And He said to them, 'Follow Me, and I will make you fishers of men.' Immediately they left their nets and followed Him" (Matthew 4:18–20).

From this account we can learn two things about the apostle formerly known as Simon. First, Peter is easily persuaded. I'm sure Christ had a certain supernatural appeal going for him, but Peter didn't even ask to see a strategic plan for this "fishers of men" venture. Second, we see that Peter had no qualms about littering — he simply dropped his nets and moved on (this is actually an important trait to notice).

The Gospels continue to recount the experiences Peter has with Christ. First, Peter witnesses Jesus healing many sick people, including his mother-in-law (see Matthew 8:15). Later, Peter and the disciples are out at sea, and they encounter a storm. Who shows up at the most opportune time but Jesus, walking on water? We read that the disciples were terrified, but St. Peter is not so terrified that he doesn't ask, "Lord, if it is You, bid me to come to You on the water" (Matthew 14:28). Peter walks on the water and then (much like I imagine babies do when they realize they've walked too far on their own to grab a wall or a table for support), "when he saw the wind, he was afraid and began to sink" (Matthew 14:31). As Jesus caught him and delivered him to the boat, all who witnessed this worshiped Christ saying, "Truly you are the Son of God" (Mathew 14:32).

Unfazed by his impetuousness, Christ continues to call Simon and in Matthew 16:18 declares, "You are Peter, and on this rock I will build My church, and the powers of death shall not prevail against it" (Matthew 16:18). Peter, James, and John witness the Transfiguration — seeing Christ speaking with Moses and Elijah and hearing the voice from heaven say, "This is my beloved Son, with whom I am well pleased; listen to Him" (Matthew 17:5).

To put it mildly, St. Peter had a privileged seat as the drama of Christ's Incarnation unfolded. He had witnessed Christ's words and deeds in the most astounding moments of His public ministry: healings, walking *with* Christ on water, even seeing Him shine like the sun, and hearing a voice from heaven say "This is My Son."

One would think that after this, Peter would stick with Jesus. Political discomfort aside, wouldn't you stand by the guy who had pulled you out of rough waters and helped you *walk on water* back to the boat?

Yet we know that this was not what happened. Just as Christ prophesied at the Last Supper, after Jesus was arrested and as He was being struck and slapped by the scribes and the elders, Peter sat outside in the courtyard and denied even *knowing* Jesus. *Three times.* We read that he then "went out and wept bitterly" (Matthew 26:75).

As wrenching as it is to imagine Christ being denied by one of his closest friends and followers, what happens next gives us hope and shows us the power of the Holy Spirit in the life of Peter, the apostles — and even little old you and me.

-FEED MY SHEEP-

After the Resurrection of Christ, Simon Peter goes fishing with some other disciples. They are out all night and catch nothing. In the morning a man on the shore asks them if they've caught anything, advising them to cast their nets on the right side of the boat. They do, and they were not even able to haul in the amount of fish they caught. John finally recognizes Jesus, and says to Peter, "It is the Lord!" And Peter's reaction? "He put on his clothes... and sprang into the sea" (John 21:7–8).

Once again, Peter is so intent on following Jesus that he drops his nets (remember I said he was a litterbug?) and runs 100 yards to shore to encounter Christ. Breakfasting on fish, Christ gives him the opportunity to say the words that Peter had probably been longing to tell him since that moment in the courtyard, before the rooster crowed:

"'Simon, son of John, do you love Me more than these?' He said to Him, 'Yes, Lord, You know that I love You.' He said to him, 'Feed My lambs.' A second time He said to him, 'Simon, son of John, do you love Me?' He said to Him, 'Yes, Lord; You know that I love You.' He said to him, 'Tend My sheep.' He said to him the third time, 'Simon, son of John, do you love Me?' Peter was grieved because He said to him a third time, 'Do you love Me?' And he said to Him, 'Lord, You know everything; You know that I love You.' Jesus said to him, 'Feed My sheep'" (John 21:15–18).

Christ has almost completed His earthly ministry at this point, so it's somewhat comical for us to read just how "off" the apostles still are. When they all gathered with Jesus in Jerusalem, Christ instructs them "not to depart from Jerusalem, but to wait for the promise of the Father, which He said, 'you heard from Me, for John baptized with water, but before many days you shall be baptized with the Holy Spirit'" (Acts 1:4–5). Christ was telling them the plan. The apostles, who at this point still must have been euphoric that Christ was once dead and now isn't, weren't picking up what He was putting down.

Christ has told them that He was going to build His Church on the "rock" that was St. Peter. He had charged St. Peter with feeding His lambs, tending His sheep, feeding His sheep (oh, St. Peter, how many times did He need to tell you?) and now Christ was telling them to sit tight, because the third Person of the Blessed Trinity was on the way. If they thought it had been a wild ride sitting in on the Sermon on the Mount, they hadn't seen *anything* yet. The Catholic Church was about to live up to its name.

THE WORD "CATHOLIC MEANS "UNIVERSAL"; THE CHURCH "HAS BEEN SENT OUT BY CHRIST ON A MISSION TO THE WHOLE HUMAN RACE" (CATECHISM OF THE CATHOLIC CHURCH 830, 831).

These apostles, who have spent three years following the second Person of the Trinity and have just been promised the third, now asked Christ, "Lord, will You at this time restore the kingdom to Israel?" (Acts 1:6). Even though He knew this would be asked (because He's God), this had to have been a face-palm moment for Christ because at this point — after all they had witnessed — the apostles were still waiting for Christ to make a political move and put the Israelites in power (that's what "restore the kingdom" meant). They still weren't thinking heaven or a universal Church established to bring people to eternity. They were on a political mission.

Christ assures them, "You shall receive power when the Holy Spirit has come upon you; and you shall be My witnesses in Jerusalem and in all Judea and Samaria and to the end of the earth" (Acts 1:8).

And with that, Christ ascends into heaven.

It must have been a rather abrupt ending for the apostles, all poised to go out and launch a "Jesus for President" campaign. Holding our leather-bound Bibles, we can miss the gravity of this moment as we read the whole story in our neatly organized church with pews, hymnals, and a parish council that serves coffee and donuts after Mass. Two thousand years later, our Church is structured. We are "the ends of the earth," and we've been witnessed to. (Thank you, apostolic succession.)

The apostles didn't have our reassurances. They had no *leather-bound* Bibles. They had no parish council. They did not even have coffee and donuts or a place to gather. All they had were the words that Christ had spoken to them. And as we can see from their final comments, they did not fully grasp the implications of those words.

Imagine how they must have felt. Think of the biggest decisions you've had to make — paper or plastic, bangs or no bangs, trying out for the football team, who to ask to prom, what colleges to apply to — and the times that you've felt paralyzed trying to figure out what you should do.

Take that feeling and multiply it by a thousand, and that's how the apostles must have felt. What do you do when the man you've given up everything to follow tells you to wait for the Holy Spirit and then disappears into the clouds?

Apparently, you do just that.

-PENTECOST-

When I was in fourth grade, my Sunday school class was involved in the Mass for Pentecost. You know how it goes — some students get to bring up the gifts and some get to pass out hymnals at the door and some students get to read the prayer intentions. I hit the liturgical-assignment jackpot and was asked to do the second reading. I loved lectoring, so I agreed to it before looking at the Scripture I'd be proclaiming.

My mother, once again demonstrating her expertise in Scriptural matters, saw that I had been assigned the reading for Pentecost and hinted that I might not want to put this one off until the last minute. I thought she was just pulling a "mom-ism" — you know, "wear a coat," "brush your teeth," "practice your Pentecost readings." You've heard one, you've heard them all.

Then I looked at Acts 2 and realized she was right. This reading was a doozy. It must have listed a least a dozen nationalities that I had never even heard of, much less pronounced. Here's why.

Have you ever watched the opening ceremony of the Olympics, when hundreds of nations march in and everyone's speaking different languages and wearing different outfits and drinking Coca-Cola (or so the commercials tell us)?

When the disciples returned to Jerusalem, they returned to the upper room and waited, just like Christ had instructed them. On the morning of Pentecost, "devout men from every nation under heaven" gathered in Jerusalem (Acts 2:5). Much like the Olympics, the World Cup, or some metropolitan food courts, there were people from many different parts of the world gathered together, and they all spoke different languages.

As the apostles waited in the upper room, "suddenly a sound came from heaven like the rush of a mighty wind, and it filled the house where they were sitting. And there appeared to them, tongues as of fire, distributed and resting on each one of them. And they were all filled with the Holy Spirit and began to speak in other tongues, as the Spirit gave them utterance" (Acts 2:2–3).

These men who, just days before had thought Christ was preparing them for seats in His cabinet for a political takeover, were transformed by the Holy Spirit. The men who had been so fearful that they had abandoned Christ when He was arrested were empowered and immediately took to the streets proclaiming "the mighty works of God" (Acts 1:11). The amazing thing is, men from "every nation under heaven" who had gathered to hear what the apostles were saying "were bewildered, because each one heard them speaking in his own language" (Acts 1:6).

It was such a commotion that many thought they had been drinking. It's here that we get to see the definitive transformation of St. Peter. Peter, who dropped his nets to follow Jesus. Peter, whose mother-in-law was healed. Peter, who walked on water when Christ invited him. Peter, who denied Christ outside the room where He is being mocked and beaten.

Peter, who until this point had been unpredictable and impulsive, is transformed by this outpouring of the Holy Spirit. Standing with the apostles, this man who had been too afraid to acknowledge Christ to a servant girl in a courtyard now testifies to all of Jerusalem, stating, "Let this be known to you, and give ear to my words. For these men are not drunk, as you suppose, since it is only the third hour of the day; but this is what was spoken by the prophet Joel: 'And in the last days, it shall be, God declares, that I will pour out My Spirit upon all flesh'" (Acts 2:14–17).

With perfect clarity, Peter delivers the plan of salvation. That Jesus was sent by God and performed signs and wonders, that He was crucified and died but that He is more powerful than death —

because the apostles witnessed His Resurrection. Boldly, Peter declares, "Let all the house of Israel therefore know assuredly that God has made Him both Lord and Christ, this Jesus whom you crucified" (Acts 2:36).

All this coming from the man who had been too fearful to remain by the side of Christ as He was crucified. Not only was he telling the Israelites about Jesus, he was pointing out that they were the ones who crucified Him.

Where's the fear?

Moved by God's Spirit, we can change the face of the earth.

Peter was transformed. The apostles were transformed. That very first day, 3,000 more souls were transformed in Jerusalem when they were baptized and began to follow the apostles both in their teaching *and* "the breaking of bread" (Acts 2:42).

-To The Ends of The Earth-

This rag-tag bunch, with no professional experience, does, in fact, bring Christ to the ends of the known earth. They would boldly face those who persecuted them and go to remarkable lengths to bring the Gospel to what is now Europe, India, Egypt, and Asia. Just take a look at the maps at the beginning or end of your Bible. (It took me a while to realize that many Bibles have maps — they're usually in the back. Check it out — it's a neat way to place yourself in the time of Christ and the apostles). Really look at the miles these guys logged and remember that this was before planes, trains, or cars. These miles were logged on foot, on a donkey, or in a boat.

In the early days after Pentecost, when Peter and the apostles are questioned by the council in Jerusalem, a man named Gamaliel warned his fellow Pharisees: "Keep away from these men and let them alone; for if this plan or this undertaking is of men, it will fail; but if it is of God, you will not be able to overthrow them. You might even be found opposing God!" (Acts 5:38–39).

While all but St. John died a martyr's death, the message of the apostles was not defeated or overthrown. Two thousand years later, the Church founded by Christ and proclaimed by these apostles and their successors continues to work to make the Kingdom of God a reality.

-MOVED BY GOD'S SPIRIT-

St. Peter's story is our story. The Holy Spirit who descended on the apostles at Pentecost and empowered them to preach the Gospel to the ends of the earth, to face persecution and even death for the sake of the Kingdom of God, is the same Holy Spirit we received at our Baptism and whose gifts are increased and perfected at our Confirmation.

Lumen Gentium describes the Sacrament of Confirmation as the sacrament by which the Baptized "are more perfectly bound to the Church and are enriched with a special strength of the Holy Spirit. Hence, they are, as true witnesses of Christ, more strictly obliged to spread and defend the faith by word and deed" (*CCC* 1285).

Whether you received the Sacrament of Confirmation a while ago, recently, or are still preparing for it, be sure of one thing. The Sacrament of Confirmation bestows all the gifts of the Spirit on you. The Sacrament of Confirmation empowers you to be a witness to the ends of the earth. The Holy Spirit you receive is the same Holy Spirit that descended on the apostles.

The Sacrament of Confirmation is *not* your graduation.

Literally the only things *Confirmation* and *graduation* have in common are the last five letters. Oh, and both events will probably involve a reception with cake. But that's it. The similarities stop there.

As we know, graduations signify the end of some sort of educational accomplishment like high school, college, or maybe eighth grade, if your school is especially festive. (Don't mention kindergarten. I refuse to accept kindergarten graduations.) I remember the day I graduated from college. It was a bittersweet moment. I had made so many good friends that I was really going to miss. On the other hand, the four years I spent in college had been the hardest I had worked in my life. Especially my senior year — I couldn't remember the last time I had read a book that wasn't for school or had the energy to watch television at the end of the day. Then, final exams came and went in a blur, and suddenly there was no more work to do.

I walked across the stage and received my diploma, packed up my dorm room, said good-bye to my friends — and it was over.

Graduation was the end. I had earned my degree, and it was time to move on.

To understand what happens in our souls when we receive the Sacrament of Confirmation, we need to look at the descent of the Holy Spirit on the apostles at Pentecost instead of any experience or idea we may have of graduation. The apostles were empowered, comforted, consoled, and moved to change the face of the earth. And so are we. Confirmation is in no way the end. It's an outpouring of these seven gifts in our lives.

You might find this idea of changing the face of the earth exciting, or you might find it a little intimidating. It's important to clarify that this doesn't mean you have to go join the Peace Corps or be a missionary in Africa. Just be ready to say "yes."

—MARY, OUR MODEL—

St. Peter and the apostles give us a dramatic example of the transformation the Holy Spirit can work in our lives, as we see them empowered to leave the upper room and proclaim the Gospel to all of Jerusalem and the ends of the earth. Where do we start?

Mary, the Mother of God, shows us that being open to the Holy Spirit begins with a simple "yes."

We know the story well. When she was just a teenager, the Angel Gabriel appeared to her, announcing, "You will conceive in your womb and bear a son, and you shall call His name Jesus" (Luke 1:31). Mary — betrothed but not yet living with Joseph — asked, "How can this be, since I have no husband?" (Luke 1:34).

The Incarnation is the word we use to describe the fact that the Son of God became a man in order to accomplish our salvation (see CCC 461). And this incredibly important moment in our story — the moment of God becoming man to save us — all depends on a teenage girl. A devout teenage girl, a virgin betrothed to a man to whom she would have to explain a pregnancy. As grave as this sounds, Joseph wasn't her only worry — the penalty for being unmarried and pregnant was death.

Gabriel tells her, "The Holy Spirit will come upon you, and the power of the Most High will overshadow you" (Luke 1:35). Mary, aware of the many possibilities that could affect her happiness and well-being yet not knowing what the future would hold, answers, "Behold, I am the handmaid of the Lord; let it be done to me according to your word" (Luke 1:38). Giving God her "yes," Mary "made it possible for the Holy Spirit to work the miracle of all miracles: the Incarnation of God" (*YouCat*, 117).

In the life of Mary — in her openness to the will of God and her "yes" that changed everything — we see every gift of the Holy Spirit. Wisdom, understanding, counsel, fortitude, knowledge, piety, and fear of the Lord are received and — without sin to obstruct them — lived perfectly.

Mary shows us that the work of the Holy Spirit in our lives begins with a "yes." We may not fully understand the question, but we can be confident that if God is asking, we will be empowered to do what we are unable to do on our own.

–WHAT I COULDN'T DO–

A few months after my college graduation, I boarded a plane to go to Belize, Central America, to live in that three-bedroom bungalow with no mirrors. My last semester in school I had taken a short mission trip there, and God asked me to come back.

It wasn't audible — but the question was posed to me in my heart as an irresistible pull that I was sure, after a lot of prayer and discussion with trusted spiritual advisors, was from God. While the consequences of my "yes" were not nearly as important as Mary's, this was the first time I acted based not on what made sense but on what I knew I was being called to do.

The night before I boarded the plane I lay in bed. My bags were packed, my alarm was set and tears were rolling down my cheeks.

I was terrified.

While Belize is certainly not the most hostile place for a first-world gal like myself, I knew it was going to hold its share of challenges for me. My biggest fears were the lizards, bugs, spiders, and mold that were common. I liked my inside spaces air-conditioned and free of any wildlife. I didn't even like to look at lizards and snakes through glass... I knew that life there was going to shatter my comfort zone.

But I was very sure that God was calling me. I didn't know why — there were crunchy granola types that owned hemp clothing and eco sandals who would have been much better suited for this endeavor. There were plenty of jobs that I could be starting in the United States that paid more than $12 a week. Nothing about me, a girl who had worked summers in an air-conditioned Gap, going to Central America made sense. Except for the very important fact that God had asked me to go, and I was trusting He had a reason.

The first 24 hours held every fear I had imagined and some I hadn't. On the way to our house, the priest who picked us up told us about a volunteer who had already left (after only a week) because a cockroach had fallen on him while he slept. When I went to use the toilet in our bungalow, there was a gecko crawling on the seat. Entering the kitchen the next morning, the housekeeper was drowning a bat she had caught inside the house that morning. One of the seminarians at the mission greeted me as I poured my coffee. He was holding a bucket covered by a lid. "Good morning! Wanna see the tarantula I just found in the church?"

Uh, no.

Over the next several weeks the challenges didn't disappear but I had never been so aware that I was not functioning on my own. Reflecting on that time I know it was the Holy Spirit that was empowering me to do what I thought I couldn't do, whether that meant calmly shaking the ants out of my clothes when I awoke to an infestation or not shrieking when a gecko ran over my foot in the shower.

Several months after my arrival, I walked into my bedroom and found a spider the size of my fist crawling across my pillow. I didn't even flinch; I just reached for my camera so I could document the experience before it disappeared into my sheets. As I tried to get the best light without scaring it away, it occurred to me just how much I had changed — all because I said "yes" when God asked me to follow Him.

-YOUR TURN-

Overcoming my fear of nature is a silly example, but when I read about St. Peter and the Blessed Mother, it gives me a glimpse into the Holy Spirit's action in the church. I know that I couldn't have stayed in Belize on my own strength. I probably couldn't even have gotten on the plane. Yet, when I took the first steps to follow and said "yes" to the invitation, I found that, while I still didn't have the strength, through the gifts of the Holy Spirit, God gave me all I needed.

This was several years after I received the Sacrament of Confirmation. Fortunately, the gifts of the Holy Spirit don't come with an expiration date. They're ready and waiting when you're ready to say "yes."

—WE NEED EACH OTHER—

In a private revelation to St. Catherine of Siena, God shared, "I have given many gifts and graces, both spiritual and temporal, with such diversity that I have not given everything to one single person, so that you may be constrained to practice charity towards one another... I have willed that one should need another and that all should be my ministers in distributing the graces and gifts they have received from Me" (*CCC* 1937).

Remember how disappointing the game Mousetrap was to me when I was six? By contrast, one of the best gifts I received as a child was a dollhouse that Santa had brought my sisters and me. It was really a beauty — complete with a family of dolls and meticulously crafted furniture for each room. I still remember the bunk beds with little blankets for the doll-children and a bathroom with a porcelain tub and teeny-tiny toilet. It even had a Christmas tree in the middle of the living room.

The dollhouse remained in the center of our playroom for years, and each birthday and Christmas our collection would expand. Our parents — and uh, Santa Claus — must have observed how the more dolls and accessories we received, the more we played with them and with each other. We'd even make our own doll accessories out of things that were never intended to be used that way — shoe boxes were stacked to make a doll apartment building, washcloths were confiscated from the bathroom to be made into doll blankets and the animals from the Christmas manger scene were kidnapped so our doll family could start a 4-H club.

What does this have to do with the message received by St. Catherine of Siena? One of the beautiful things about humanity is that while we are all gifted, we're also all different. Our natural talents and abilities mean that the Holy Spirit working in our lives — while serving us all in our journey to heaven — will look a little different in each of us and, more importantly, provides an opportunity for us to serve one another.

When my sisters and I received the dollhouse for Christmas, it brought us together and continued to do so with each new accessory or doll to play with. When I received a doll bicycle, my sister was excited because she could play with it, too. When my sister received a doll camper, I knew that meant the whole doll family would be able to now go on a camping trip. A gift for one of us was a gift for all, and when we sought to improve the gifts (like our shoebox apartment or wash cloth blankets), we all benefited.

(I realize this doll analogy might be lost on some. If you were never into dolls, maybe you can apply that same story to G.I. Joes or an Xbox.)

The point is that gifts of the Holy Spirit working in your life are not just for you. The gifts of wisdom, understanding, counsel, fortitude, knowledge, piety, and fear of the Lord are given first to you — but as we can see from the lives of the saints and holy people in our lives — they are gifts for our Church, to build up the body of Christ and help us all on our journey to heaven.

The Holy Spirit that overshadowed Mary and allowed her to cooperate with our redemption, the Holy Spirit that empowered the apostles to bring the Gospel to the ends of the earth — this is the Holy Spirit that we have. These are the gifts we have been given.

Using them is up to you.